# God Hears Her

## 40-DAY DEVOTIONAL JOURNAL

**Our Daily Bread**
Publishing™

# HOW TO USE THIS BOOK

The women writers of *Our Daily Bread* are so glad to welcome you into these pages. We invite you to grow with us as we dig into and plant ourselves in the truth that *God hears us*. Through Scripture, *God Hears Her* devotionals, and journaling prompts, we will explore what it means that the Almighty Creator of the universe—our Comforter and Sustainer, our Father God— hears us. He hears *you*.

The journaling prompts will help open your eyes to God's work in your life. They'll direct you to immerse yourself in Scripture and personalize what God is saying to you through it. They'll draw you into worship and praise. They'll lead you to gut-wrenching, soul-baring honesty. And they'll remind you that He's listening.

Join us for forty days and draw closer to God as He draws closer to you. Be reminded every day: God is with you and God is for you.

# 1 SAMUEL 1:9-20

Once when they had finished eating and drinking in Shiloh, Hannah stood up. Now Eli the priest was sitting on his chair by the doorpost of the LORD's house. In her deep anguish Hannah prayed to the LORD, weeping bitterly. And she made a vow, saying, "LORD Almighty, if you will only look on your servant's misery and remember me, and not forget your servant but give her a son, then I will give him to the LORD for all the days of his life, and no razor will ever be used on his head."

As she kept on praying to the LORD, Eli observed her mouth. Hannah was praying in her heart, and her lips were moving but her voice was not heard. Eli thought she was drunk and said to her, "How long are you going to stay drunk? Put away your wine."

"Not so, my lord," Hannah replied, "I am a woman who is deeply troubled. I have not been drinking wine or beer; I was pouring out my soul to the LORD. Do not take your servant for a wicked woman; I have been praying here out of my great anguish and grief."

Eli answered, "Go in peace, and may the God of Israel grant you what you have asked of him."

She said, "May your servant find favor in your eyes." Then she went her way and ate something, and her face was no longer downcast.

Early the next morning they arose and worshiped before the LORD and then went back to their home at Ramah. Elkanah made love to his wife Hannah, and the LORD remembered her. So in the course of time Hannah became pregnant and gave birth to a son. She named him Samuel, saying, "Because I asked the LORD for him."

The all-knowing God
hears my every prayer—
even silent ones.

## GOD HEARS HER

One day I told my daughter I was going to read a grown-up book for a while, and then we would look at books together. When I started to read in silence, she looked at me and said, "Mommy, you aren't really reading." If I wasn't speaking, she assumed I wasn't processing words.

Like reading, prayer can be silent. The Old Testament character Hannah, who longed for a child, visited the temple and prayed "in her heart." Her lips were moving, but "her voice was not heard" (1 Samuel 1:13). She explained, "I was pouring out my soul to the LORD" (v. 15). God heard Hannah's silent prayer and gave her a son (v. 20).

Our all-knowing God searches our hearts and minds, and He hears every prayer—even silent ones. We can confidently pray—knowing He'll hear and answer (Matthew 6:8, 32). We can praise God, ask Him for help, and thank Him for blessings—even when no one else can hear us. If someone sees us talking to the Lord, he or she can say with confidence: "God hears her!"

*Jennifer*

Hannah was praying in her
heart, and her lips were moving
but her voice was not heard.

1 SAMUEL 1:13

# CONNECT

Hannah felt alone and desperate about her situation. But when Hannah prayed in her heart, "the Lᴏʀᴅ remembered her" (1 Samuel 1:19) and blessed her with a child. When have you felt as if God wasn't listening? How has He shown you that He really does hear you?

## PRAY

Talk to God about your deepest desire.

Read 1 Samuel 1:9–20 again, and enter into the biblical story by imagining yourself as Hannah. Take part in each unfolding scene: What do you touch or taste or smell? Who do you talk to? How do their words make you feel? As you experience Hannah's desire for a child, what desires of your own come up? Take time to voice them to God.

*Write*

# Day 1

## MATTHEW 11:25-30 NRSV

At that time Jesus said, "I thank you, Father, Lord of heaven and earth, because you have hidden these things from the wise and the intelligent and have revealed them to infants; yes, Father, for such was your gracious will. All things have been handed over to me by my Father; and no one knows the Son except the Father, and no one knows the Father except the Son and anyone to whom the Son chooses to reveal him.

"Come to me, all you that are weary and are carrying heavy burdens, and I will give you rest. Take my yoke upon you, and learn from me; for I am gentle and humble in heart, and you will find rest for your souls. For my yoke is easy, and my burden is light."

Jesus gives me rest.

## "COME TO ME"

I was stressed about mounting medical bills after we had our third daughter. I couldn't sleep as I tried to figure out how we'd pay the bills. My muscles were tense. I was exhausted. So I cried out to God.

Experts tell us to combat stress by getting plenty of rest, eating right, and exercising. But Jesus tells us about something else that provides true peace and rest: prayer.

As I prayed, I was reminded of Matthew 11:28 where Jesus said, "Come to me, all you who are weary and burdened, and I will give you rest." Jesus invited me to come to Him to gain perspective and real rest. In the next verse, He said, "Take my yoke upon you and learn from me . . . and you will find rest for your souls" (v. 29). Our loving Savior doesn't scold us for being unable to handle the pressures of life by ourselves. Instead, He wants us to *give* our burdens to Him (Psalm 55:22).

Go to Him today!

Marlena

# PRAY

Identify a heavy burden you carry (v. 29),
and bring it to Jesus.

# CONNECT

Quiet yourself and hear Jesus's words: "Come to me, all you that are weary and are carrying heavy burdens, and I will give you rest. Take my yoke upon you, and learn from me; for I am gentle and humble in heart, and you will find rest for your souls. For my yoke is easy, and my burden is light" (vv. 28–29). What is Christ's invitation to you through these words? What do you particularly need to hold on to right now?

# Take Inventory

What current activities and experiences are life-giving to you? Which are draining your energy? Share them here.

* ............................................................................
............................................................................
............................................................................

* ............................................................................
............................................................................
............................................................................

* ............................................................................
............................................................................
............................................................................

* ............................................................................
............................................................................
............................................................................

* ............................................................................
............................................................................
............................................................................

Come to me, all
you that are weary
and are carrying
heavy burdens,
and I will
give you rest.

MATTHEW 11:28 NRSV

Day 3

# EPHESIANS 1:3-10 NLT

All praise to God, the Father of our Lord Jesus Christ, who has blessed us with every spiritual blessing in the heavenly realms because we are united with Christ. Even before he made the world, God loved us and chose us in Christ to be holy and without fault in his eyes. God decided in advance to adopt us into his own family by bringing us to himself through Jesus Christ. This is what he wanted to do, and it gave him great pleasure. So we praise God for the glorious grace he has poured out on us who belong to his dear Son. He is so rich in kindness and grace that he purchased our freedom with the blood of his Son and forgave our sins. He has showered his kindness on us, along with all wisdom and understanding.

God has now revealed to us his mysterious will regarding Christ—which is to fulfill his own good plan. And this is the plan: At the right time he will bring everything together under the authority of Christ—everything in heaven and on earth.

# God's favor is a gift.

## JUST THE TICKET

When a police officer stopped a woman because her young daughter was riding in a car without the required booster seat, he could have written her a ticket. Instead, he asked to meet the mother and daughter at a nearby store where he bought them the needed car seat. It was something the struggling mother couldn't have purchased on her own.

Although the woman should have received a fine, she walked away with a gift instead. Anyone who knows Christ has experienced something similar. All of us deserve a penalty for breaking God's laws (Ecclesiastes 7:20). Yet because of Jesus, we experience undeserved favor from God. This favor excuses us from the ultimate consequence for our sin. "In [Jesus] we have . . . the forgiveness of sins, in accordance with the riches of God's grace" (Ephesians 1:7).

When the young mother experienced this, she later remarked, "I will be forever grateful!" This response to the officer's gift is an inspiring example for those of us who have received the gift of God's grace!

*Jennifer*

Remember a time when you or your family's needs were met so completely (and generously!) you knew it had nothing to do with you—God must have been behind it! Take time to reflect on the experience, praising God for the gift.

He is so rich in kindness and grace that he purchased our freedom with the blood of his Son and forgave our sins.

EPHESIANS 1:7 NLT

Choose one of the gifts in your life. It could be a responsibility, a talent, a circumstance, a relationship . . . Journal why you are thankful for this gift.

*Write*

........................................................................................................

........................................................................................................

........................................................................................................

........................................................................................................

........................................................................................................

........................................................................................................

........................................................................................................

........................................................................................................

........................................................................................................

........................................................................................................

## PRAY

Identify where you need God to move in big or small ways in your life or in the lives of those you love.

# 1 CORINTHIANS 9:24-27 NLT

Don't you realize that in a race everyone runs, but only one person gets the prize? So run to win! All athletes are disciplined in their training. They do it to win a prize that will fade away, but we do it for an eternal prize. So I run with purpose in every step. I am not just shadowboxing. I discipline my body like an athlete, training it to do what it should. Otherwise, I fear that after preaching to others I myself might be disqualified.

*I train my heart and mind—*
*making a space for God's*
*transforming work in me.*

## ᴛRAINING FOR LIFE

I met a woman who has pushed her body and mind to the limit. She climbed mountains, faced death, and even broke a Guinness world record. Now she's engaged in a different challenge—raising her special-needs child. The courage and faith she employed while ascending the mountains she now pours into motherhood.

In 1 Corinthians, the apostle Paul speaks of a runner competing in a race. After urging a church full of people who were in love with their own rights to begin showing consideration for each other (chapter 8), he explains that he saw the challenges of love and self-sacrifice to be like a marathon of endurance (chapter 9). As followers of Jesus, they were to relinquish their rights in obedience to Him.

As athletes train their bodies to win, we can train our bodies and minds so our souls can flourish. As we ask the Holy Spirit to transform us, we leave our old selves behind. Empowered by God, we stop ourselves from actions that are not godly.

As we train ourselves in the Spirit of Christ, how might God want to mold us today?

*Amy*

## Take part in an activity that nourishes your soul this week.

With all the pressures we face today, saying no can be a spiritual exercise. Even our heavenly Father created Sabbath—a day He could rest from work (Genesis 2:2-3)! Where in your life do you need to practice the spiritual discipline of saying no?

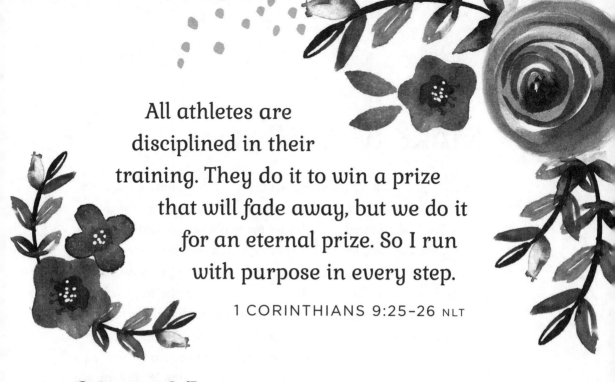

All athletes are disciplined in their training. They do it to win a prize that will fade away, but we do it for an eternal prize. So I run with purpose in every step.

1 CORINTHIANS 9:25–26 NLT

## CONNECT

In your Bible reading today, the apostle Paul says growing in faith is like training for a race. What are some ways you can "train" for this race of faith?

# MARK 5:24-34 NRSV

And a large crowd followed him and pressed in on him. Now there was a woman who had been suffering from hemorrhages for twelve years. She had endured much under many physicians, and had spent all that she had; and she was no better, but rather grew worse. She had heard about Jesus, and came up behind him in the crowd and touched his cloak, for she said, "If I but touch his clothes, I will be made well." Immediately her hemorrhage stopped; and she felt in her body that she was healed of her disease. Immediately aware that power had gone forth from him, Jesus turned about in the crowd and said, "Who touched my clothes?" And his disciples said to him, "You see the crowd pressing in on you; how can you say, 'Who touched me?'" He looked all around to see who had done it. But the woman, knowing what had happened to her, came in fear and trembling, fell down before him, and told him the whole truth. He said to her, "Daughter, your faith has made you well; go in peace, and be healed of your disease."

My need moves God's heart.

## Holy Desperation

When Jesus stood in the midst of the crowd and asked who had touched Him, the disciples must have thought He had lost it. So many people pressed in, yet He wanted to identify just one (Mark 5:31). Eventually, the woman trembled forward with a confession, stunning everyone (5:33).

Jesus knew this woman needed Him. Doctors had drained her resources, and the nonstop bleeding condemned her to be unclean. To avoid contamination, family and friends had to keep away. She couldn't enter the temple. And this had been going on for twelve years! Jesus was her only hope (Mark 5:26–28). So she touched Him. And He knew it.

How do we "touch" Him? Do we approach God with the understanding that He's our only hope? Or do we come carelessly, browsing for blessings?

In Isaiah 29:13 and Matthew 15:8, the Scriptures address the problem of making a verbal show of faith without a true heart commitment. Jesus sees past the façade to what lies beneath. With true sincerity and in dire need, let's seek Him and His loving touch today.

*Remi*

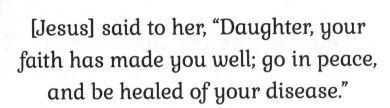

[Jesus] said to her, "Daughter, your faith has made you well; go in peace, and be healed of your disease."

MARK 5:34 NRSV

# CONNECT

In the story found in Mark 5:24–34, Jesus sees the woman as well as her needs, and He heals her. In what ways has God met your needs and answered your prayers? Praise and thank Him for His faithfulness to you!

Ask Jesus to move on your behalf in an area of need.

Read Mark 5:24–34 from the perspective of the woman who meets Jesus. When you hear Jesus is coming to your hometown, why do you hope for healing after every treatment has failed you? As you make your way to Jesus, what do you hear, see, and touch? Take hold of Jesus's cloak, and experience His healing and His loving words for you.

*Write*

.....................................................................................................................

.....................................................................................................................

.....................................................................................................................

.....................................................................................................................

.....................................................................................................................

.....................................................................................................................

.....................................................................................................................

.....................................................................................................................

.....................................................................................................................

# PSALM 37:3-11 NRSV

Trust in the LORD, and do good;

  so you will live in the land, and enjoy security.

Take delight in the LORD,

  and he will give you the desires of your heart.

Commit your way to the LORD;

  trust in him, and he will act.

He will make your vindication shine like the light,

  and the justice of your cause like the noonday.

Be still before the LORD, and wait patiently for him;

  do not fret over those who prosper in their way,

  over those who carry out evil devices.

Refrain from anger, and forsake wrath.

  Do not fret—it leads only to evil.

For the wicked shall be cut off,

  but those who wait for the LORD shall inherit the land.

Yet a little while, and the wicked will be no more;

  though you look diligently for their place, they will not be there.

But the meek shall inherit the land,

  and delight themselves in abundant prosperity.

God fulfills His
dreams for me when
the timing is right.

# TIMING IS EVERYTHING

What I thought was a coincidental meeting had been good timing on my future husband's part.

From the balcony of the church, he had seen me, deduced which exit I might be using, raced down two flights of stairs, and arrived seconds before I did. As he casually held the door and struck up a conversation, I was oblivious to the fact that his "impromptu" dinner invitation had been premeditated. It was perfect timing.

Perfect timing is rare—at least where humans are concerned. But God has specific purposes and plans for us, and His timing is always perfect.

We see that timing in the life of Bible characters: Abraham's servant prayed for a wife for Isaac. God answered his prayer by bringing the young woman to him (Genesis 24). And we marvel at Esther's courage as Mordecai reminded her, "Who knows but that you have come to your royal position for such a time as this?" (Esther 4:14).

Disappointed in the pace of God's plans? "Trust in the LORD" (Psalm 37:3). God will open doors when the timing is perfect.

*Cindy*

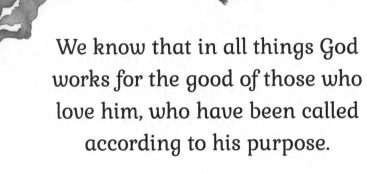

We know that in all things God works for the good of those who love him, who have been called according to his purpose.

ROMANS 8:28

# CONNECT

When has God worked to bring things together for your good (Romans 8:28)?

## PRAY

Praise God for the way He is working on your behalf, even if it's invisible to you right now.

Is God growing a dream in your heart? What is it, and why are you excited to be pursuing this vision with Him? If you're still waiting for the dream to take shape, how is God preparing you in the meantime? Talk with God about His dreams and His desires for you.

*Write*

# HABAKKUK 1:1-4 NLT

This is the message that the prophet Habakkuk received in a vision.

How long, O LORD, must I call for help?
> But you do not listen!
"Violence is everywhere!" I cry,
> but you do not come to save.
Must I forever see these evil deeds?
> Why must I watch all this misery?
Wherever I look,
> I see destruction and violence.
I am surrounded by people
> who love to argue and fight.
The law has become paralyzed,
> and there is no justice in the courts.
The wicked far outnumber the righteous,
> so that justice has become perverted.

# I can be honest with God in prayer.

## ─ How Long, God? ─

Not long ago I was certain God was moving my husband and me in a specific direction. We were encouraged and excited, for what we never thought would happen was coming together right before our very eyes. As we bathed the process in prayer, God seemed to be honoring our requests. Until the eleventh hour. That's when the door was slammed shut in our faces. We were shocked.

*Why would you do this to us, God? Why lead us on?* We felt like the prophet Habakkuk who complained to the Lord, "How long, Lord, must I call for help, but you do not listen?" (Habakkuk 1:2). Like Habakkuk's two "complaints" found in chapters 1 and 2, it was good for us to be honest with God. He knew our questions and complaints.

Habakkuk, despite his questions, could state, "Yet I will rejoice in the Lord. . . . The Sovereign Lord is my strength" (Habakkuk 3:18–19). God is still good, even when circumstances are not.

*Marlena*

# CONNECT

Describe a time in your life when you thought God was leading you one way, only to have the door closed to that opportunity. How did that feel? Talk with God about your experience.

How long,
O Lord, must I
call for help?
But you
do not listen!

HABAKKUK 1:2 NLT

Sometimes Jesus feels absent when we need Him most. In your imagination, return to a situation in which Jesus felt distant. Imagine the scene: the who, what, when, and where. As you look around in your memory, ask Jesus to show you where He was present in that circumstance.

*Write*

........................................................................................

........................................................................................

........................................................................................

........................................................................................

........................................................................................

........................................................................................

........................................................................................

........................................................................................

........................................................................................

## PRAY

As the prophet Habakkuk did, express your doubt, anger, fear, or joy openly with Jesus.

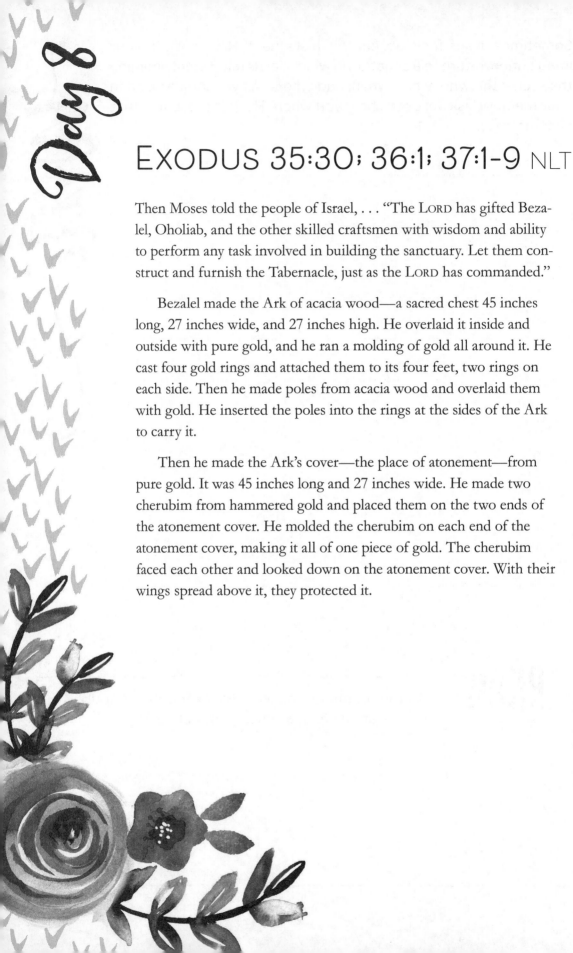

# EXODUS 35:30; 36:1; 37:1-9 NLT

Then Moses told the people of Israel, . . . "The LORD has gifted Bezalel, Oholiab, and the other skilled craftsmen with wisdom and ability to perform any task involved in building the sanctuary. Let them construct and furnish the Tabernacle, just as the LORD has commanded."

Bezalel made the Ark of acacia wood—a sacred chest 45 inches long, 27 inches wide, and 27 inches high. He overlaid it inside and outside with pure gold, and he ran a molding of gold all around it. He cast four gold rings and attached them to its four feet, two rings on each side. Then he made poles from acacia wood and overlaid them with gold. He inserted the poles into the rings at the sides of the Ark to carry it.

Then he made the Ark's cover—the place of atonement—from pure gold. It was 45 inches long and 27 inches wide. He made two cherubim from hammered gold and placed them on the two ends of the atonement cover. He molded the cherubim on each end of the atonement cover, making it all of one piece of gold. The cherubim faced each other and looked down on the atonement cover. With their wings spread above it, they protected it.

*I experience God
through my five senses.*

# THE SENSUOUS CHRISTIAN

The gratification of our senses has gotten a bad reputation, perhaps because we live in a world obsessed with pleasure. But God approves of the proper experience of pleasure through our five senses.

First, God created our senses—sight, hearing, smell, taste, touch—and all that He created is good.

Second, God made sensuousness a part of worship. Consider God's first formal worship setting: the tabernacle. It housed an ornate, gold-covered ark to hold the stone tablets God gave to Moses on Mount Sinai. God approves of beauty. Around the tabernacle were curtains made from colorful yarn and finely twisted linen. God approves of beautiful colors and textures. Music was also a component of worship, as we learn from reading 2 Chronicles 29:28. God approves of pleasing sounds.

Yes, God values things that look, sound, smell, taste, and feel good. But He doesn't want us to worship them; He wants our enjoyment and gratitude to prompt us to worship Him, the Creator and giver of all good things.

*Julie*

Pay attention to what you experience
via your five senses today.

# CONNECT

In our broken world, beauty is often misused or abused—twisting our relationship with something God created *very good*. What is your relationship with beauty? Is it healthy, or what keeps you from having a healthy view of beauty?

# Take Inventory

How has God wired you to see beauty in the world around you? What things that you touch, smell, taste, see, or hear give you joy?

Every good and perfect gift is from above, coming down from the Father of the heavenly lights, who does not change like shifting shadows.

JAMES 1:17

*

*

*

*

*

# MARK 9:14-27

When they came to the other disciples, they saw a large crowd around them and the teachers of the law arguing with them. As soon as all the people saw Jesus, they were overwhelmed with wonder and ran to greet him.

"What are you arguing with them about?" he asked.

A man in the crowd answered, "Teacher, I brought you my son, who is possessed by a spirit that has robbed him of speech. Whenever it seizes him, it throws him to the ground. He foams at the mouth, gnashes his teeth and becomes rigid. I asked your disciples to drive out the spirit, but they could not."

"You unbelieving generation," Jesus replied, "how long shall I stay with you? How long shall I put up with you? Bring the boy to me."

So they brought him. When the spirit saw Jesus, it immediately threw the boy into a convulsion. He fell to the ground and rolled around, foaming at the mouth.

Jesus asked the boy's father, "How long has he been like this?"

"From childhood," he answered. "It has often thrown him into fire or water to kill him. But if you can do anything, take pity on us and help us."

"'If you can'?" said Jesus. "Everything is possible for one who believes."

Immediately the boy's father exclaimed, "I do believe; help me overcome my unbelief!"

When Jesus saw that a crowd was running to the scene, he rebuked the impure spirit. "You deaf and mute spirit," he said, "I command you, come out of him and never enter him again."

The spirit shrieked, convulsed him violently and came out. The boy looked so much like a corpse that many said, "He's dead." But Jesus took him by the hand and lifted him to his feet, and he stood up.

# God invites me to release my burdens to Him.

## "BRING THE BOY TO ME"

"I don't believe in God, and I won't go," Mark said.

Amy struggled to swallow the lump in her throat. Her son had changed from a happy boy to a surly, uncooperative young man. Life was a battleground, and Sunday had become a day to dread, as Mark refused to go to church with the family. Finally, his despairing parents consulted a counselor, who said, "Mark must make his own faith journey. You can't force him into the kingdom. Give God space to work. Keep praying, and wait."

Amy waited—and prayed. One morning the words of Jesus that she had read echoed through her mind. Jesus's disciples had failed to help a demon-possessed boy, but Jesus had the answer: "Bring the boy to me" (Mark 9:19). If Jesus could heal in such an extreme situation, surely He could also help her son. She mentally stepped back, leaving her son alone with the One who loved him even more than she did.

Every day Amy silently handed Mark to God, clinging to the assurance that He knew Mark's needs and would in His time and in His way work in his life.

*Marion*

"You unbelieving generation,"
Jesus replied, "how long shall I stay
with you? How long shall I put up with
you? Bring the boy to me."

MARK 9:19

## CONNECT

In Mark 9:23, Jesus said, "Everything is possible for one who believes."
What are some impossible things that you could pray to God about?

## Imagine offloading your heaviest burden to Christ.

Jesus loves when we are honest with Him. In Mark 9:21–24, a father asks Jesus to heal his son but doubts that Jesus can heal him: "I do believe; help me overcome my unbelief!" (v. 24). Moved by the confession, Jesus heals the boy. Where are you struggling to trust God? Make the father's words your own, and share your faith and your fears with Jesus.

*Write*

........................................................................................................

........................................................................................................

........................................................................................................

........................................................................................................

........................................................................................................

........................................................................................................

........................................................................................................

........................................................................................................

........................................................................................................

# Day 10

## JOHN 16:16-22 NLT

"In a little while you won't see me anymore. But a little while after that, you will see me again."

Some of the disciples asked each other, "What does he mean when he says, 'In a little while you won't see me, but then you will see me,' and 'I am going to the Father'? And what does he mean by 'a little while'? We don't understand."

Jesus realized they wanted to ask him about it, so he said, "Are you asking yourselves what I meant? I said in a little while you won't see me, but a little while after that you will see me again. I tell you the truth, you will weep and mourn over what is going to happen to me, but the world will rejoice. You will grieve, but your grief will suddenly turn to wonderful joy. It will be like a woman suffering the pains of labor. When her child is born, her anguish gives way to joy because she has brought a new baby into the world. So you have sorrow now, but I will see you again; then you will rejoice, and no one can rob you of that joy."

## The Holy Spirit helps me to feel joy even in an imperfect world.

# — FROM GRIEF TO JOY —

Kelly's pregnancy brought complications, and doctors were concerned. During her long labor, they decided to whisk her away for a Caesarean section. But despite the ordeal, Kelly quickly forgot her pain when she held her newborn son. Joy had replaced anguish.

Scripture affirms this truth: "A woman giving birth to a child has pain because her time has come; but when her baby is born she forgets the anguish because of her joy" (John 16:21). Jesus used this illustration with His disciples to emphasize that though they would grieve His soon departure, that grief would turn to joy when they saw Him again (vv. 20–22).

Jesus was referring to His death and resurrection—and what followed. When Jesus ascended into heaven, He did not leave His friends grief-stricken. He sent the Holy Spirit, who would fill them with joy (John 16:7–15; Acts 13:52).

When someday we see Jesus face-to-face, the anguish we experience on this earth will be forgotten. But until then, the Lord has not left us without joy—He has given us His Spirit (Romans 15:13; 1 Peter 1:8–9).

*Alyson*

# CONNECT

Jesus uses the analogy of a woman giving birth to describe how joy follows pain and suffering. Can you think of any other images or analogies that can remind us of this transformation?

You will grieve,
but your grief will
suddenly turn to
wonderful joy.

JOHN 16:20 NLT

What would you like to be made new in heaven—maybe a broken relationship, a loss, a circumstance beyond your control? Talk with Jesus about your hopes.

*Write*

....................................................................................................

....................................................................................................

....................................................................................................

....................................................................................................

....................................................................................................

....................................................................................................

....................................................................................................

....................................................................................................

....................................................................................................

Think of an area of your life that has been restored—and then one yet-to-be restored.

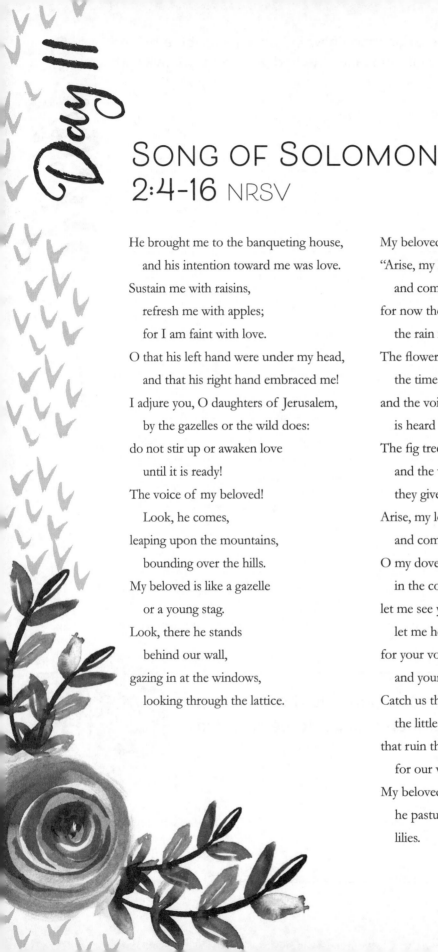

# SONG OF SOLOMON
## 2:4-16 NRSV

He brought me to the banqueting house,
  and his intention toward me was love.
Sustain me with raisins,
  refresh me with apples;
  for I am faint with love.
O that his left hand were under my head,
  and that his right hand embraced me!
I adjure you, O daughters of Jerusalem,
  by the gazelles or the wild does:
do not stir up or awaken love
  until it is ready!
The voice of my beloved!
  Look, he comes,
leaping upon the mountains,
  bounding over the hills.
My beloved is like a gazelle
  or a young stag.
Look, there he stands
  behind our wall,
gazing in at the windows,
  looking through the lattice.

My beloved speaks and says to me:
"Arise, my love, my fair one,
  and come away;
for now the winter is past,
  the rain is over and gone.
The flowers appear on the earth;
  the time of singing has come,
and the voice of the turtledove
  is heard in our land.
The fig tree puts forth its figs,
  and the vines are in blossom;
  they give forth fragrance.
Arise, my love, my fair one,
  and come away.
O my dove, in the clefts of the rock,
  in the covert of the cliff,
let me see your face,
  let me hear your voice;
for your voice is sweet,
  and your face is lovely.
Catch us the foxes,
  the little foxes,
that ruin the vineyards—
  for our vineyards are in blossom."
My beloved is mine and I am his;
  he pastures his flock among the
  lilies.

God is my Beloved.

# THE GREATEST LOVE STORY

When John and Ann Betar celebrated their eighty-first wedding anniversary, they were considered the couple with the longest marriage in the United States. Their advice? "Don't hold a grudge. Forgive each other," John advises. And Ann adds, "It is unconditional love and understanding."

The Song of Songs captures this active commitment with two lovers delighting in and yearning for each other (1:15–16; 3:1–3). They love and are loved in return (2:16; 7:10) and are satisfied and content in each other's company (2:16; 4:9–11; 7:10). Surely this can be one of life's greatest joys.

The earthly love between husband and wife is an echo of the passionate love and fervent pursuit of Jesus for those who believe in Him. "This is how God loved the world: He gave his one and only Son, so that everyone who believes in him will not perish but have eternal life" (John 3:16 NLT).

While it's beautiful to see the love a man and woman can share for decades, it pales compared to the amazing love God extends to us for eternity. *That's* the greatest love story!

*Ruth*

My beloved is mine
and I am his.

SONG OF SOLOMON 2:16 NRSV

## CONNECT

How has God's unchanging love for you freed you to grow or to take a risk?

# PRAY

Give Jesus, your Beloved, permission to delight in you
(Zephaniah 3:14, 17).

Imagine Song of Solomon 2:4–16 is a love poem between you and God. As you read it, stop at a phrase that captures your imagination—for example, "arise, my love" (v. 10) or "my beloved is mine" (v. 16). Sit with that phrase for your entire prayer time, listening to God's personal invitation for you.

*Write*

# JOHN 13:31-35 NLT

As soon as Judas left the room, Jesus said, "The time has come for the Son of Man to enter into his glory, and God will be glorified because of him. And since God receives glory because of the Son, he will give his own glory to the Son, and he will do so at once. Dear children, I will be with you only a little longer. And as I told the Jewish leaders, you will search for me, but you can't come where I am going. So now I am giving you a new commandment: Love each other. Just as I have loved you, you should love each other. Your love for one another will prove to the world that you are my disciples."

> Knowing Christ
> leads to caring for the
> people in our world.

## A WONDERFUL EXPLOSION

In the book *Kisses from Katie*, Katie Davis recounts the joy of moving to Uganda and adopting several Ugandan girls. One day one of her daughters asked, "Mommy, if I let Jesus come into my heart, will I explode?" At first Katie said no.

However, after she thought more about the question, Katie explained that when we decide to give our lives and hearts to Jesus, "we will explode with love, with compassion, with hurt for those who are hurting, and with joy for those who rejoice." In essence, knowing Christ results in deep concern for the people in our world.

We can consistently display this loving response because of the Holy Spirit's work in our hearts. When we receive Christ, the Holy Spirit comes to live inside us. The apostle Paul said, "When you believed, you were marked . . . [with] the promised Holy Spirit" (Ephesians 1:13).

Caring for others—with God's supernatural assistance—shows the world we are His followers (John 13:35). This also reminds us of His love for us. Jesus said, "As I have loved you, so you must love one another" (v. 34).

*Jennifer*

Where is God nudging you to learn more about an issue or cause, to use your gifts in service of others, or to give generously?

> So now I am giving you a new commandment: Love each other. Just as I have loved you, you should love each other.

JOHN 13:34 NLT

Think of someone who has extraordinarily influenced your life. Write an imaginary letter to this person: Tell them what they mean to you, and how they have changed your life. Thank them for the gift they are to you!

*Write*

..........................................................................................................

..........................................................................................................

..........................................................................................................

..........................................................................................................

..........................................................................................................

..........................................................................................................

..........................................................................................................

..........................................................................................................

..........................................................................................................

## PRAY

*Jesus, move my heart for the things that move your own.*

# LUKE 18:9-14

To some who were confident of their own righteousness and looked down on everyone else, Jesus told this parable: "Two men went up to the temple to pray, one a Pharisee and the other a tax collector. The Pharisee stood by himself and prayed: 'God, I thank you that I am not like other people—robbers, evildoers, adulterers—or even like this tax collector. I fast twice a week and give a tenth of all I get.'

"But the tax collector stood at a distance. He would not even look up to heaven, but beat his breast and said, 'God, have mercy on me, a sinner.'

"I tell you that this man, rather than the other, went home justified before God. For all those who exalt themselves will be humbled, and those who humble themselves will be exalted."

# I bring my own sin before God instead of criticizing others.

## PRAYER CIRCLES

Around the circle the sixth-grade girls went, taking turns praying for each other. "Father in heaven," Anna prayed, "please help Tonya not to be so boy crazy." Tonya added with a giggle, "And help Anna to stop acting so horrible in school." Then Talia prayed, "Lord, help Tonya to listen to her mother instead of always talking back."

Although the requests were real, the girls seemed to enjoy teasing their friends by pointing out their flaws in prayer. Their group leader reminded them about the seriousness of talking to almighty God and the importance of evaluating their own hearts.

If we use prayer to point out the faults of others while ignoring our own, we're like the Pharisee in Jesus's parable. He prayed, "God, I thank you that I am not like other people—robbers, evildoers, adulterers" (Luke 18:11). Instead, we're to be like the man who asked God to be merciful to him, "a sinner" (v. 13).

The kind of prayer God desires from us flows out of a humble evaluation of our own sinful hearts.

*Anne*

Voice the tax collector's prayer from Luke 18:13:
*God, have mercy on me, a sinner.*

Where am I growing in vulnerability and honesty with others and God? Where am I hiding from others and God?

Write

......................................................................................

......................................................................................

......................................................................................

......................................................................................

......................................................................................

......................................................................................

......................................................................................

......................................................................................

......................................................................................

......................................................................................

Those who exalt themselves will be
humbled, and those who humble
themselves will be exalted.

LUKE 18:14

# CONNECT

God gives us prayer as a way to talk to Him as a Father. What are some
ways that prayer can bless you?

# JOB 23:2-12

Even today my complaint is bitter;

    his hand is heavy in spite of my groaning.

If only I knew where to find him;

    if only I could go to his dwelling!

I would state my case before him

    and fill my mouth with arguments.

I would find out what he would answer me,

    and consider what he would say to me.

Would he vigorously oppose me?

    No, he would not press charges against me.

There the upright can establish their innocence before him,

    and there I would be delivered forever from my judge.

But if I go to the east, he is not there;

    if I go to the west, I do not find him.

When he is at work in the north, I do not see him;

    when he turns to the south, I catch no glimpse of him.

But he knows the way that I take;

    when he has tested me, I will come forth as gold.

My feet have closely followed his steps;

    I have kept to his way without turning aside.

I have not departed from the commands of his lips;

    I have treasured the words of his mouth more than my daily bread.

God can use anything in
my life—even suffering—
to help me grow.

# Tried and Purified

During an interview, singer and songwriter Meredith Andrews spoke about being overwhelmed as she tried to balance outreach, creative work, marital issues, and motherhood. Reflecting on her distress, she said, "I felt like God was taking me through a refining season—almost through a crushing process."

The Old Testament character Job was overwhelmed after losing so much. And although Job had been a daily worshiper of God, he felt that the Lord was ignoring his pleas for help. Job claimed he could not see God whether he looked to the north, south, east, or west (Job 23:2–9).

In the middle of his despair, Job had a moment of clarity. He said, "[God] knows the way that I take; when he has tested me, I will come forth as gold" (v. 10). Sometimes God uses difficulty to burn away our self-reliance, pride, and earthly wisdom.

Pain and problems can produce the shining, rock-solid character that comes from trusting God when life is hard.

*Jennifer*

When he has tested me,
I will come forth as gold.

JOB 23:10

## CONNECT

Today's reading reminds us that "God uses difficulty to burn away our self-reliance, pride, and earthly wisdom." When have you experienced this kind of burning away?

## PRAY

Ask Jesus to help a friend who is experiencing a challenging situation.

The biblical Job lost his family, his wealth, his health—suffering so extreme it's hard for us to imagine! Who in your life has struggled and pressed on with God's help? What do you admire about the way he or she faced suffering?

*Write*

# JOHN 12:1-8 NRSV

Six days before the Passover Jesus came to Bethany, the home of
Lazarus, whom he had raised from the dead. There they gave a dinner
for him. Martha served, and Lazarus was one of those at the table
with him. Mary took a pound of costly perfume made of pure nard,
anointed Jesus' feet, and wiped them with her hair. The house was
filled with the fragrance of the perfume. But Judas Iscariot, one of
his disciples (the one who was about to betray him), said, "Why was
this perfume not sold for three hundred denarii and the money given
to the poor?" (He said this not because he cared about the poor, but
because he was a thief; he kept the common purse and used to steal
what was put into it.) Jesus said, "Leave her alone. She bought it so that
she might keep it for the day of my burial. You always have the poor
with you, but you do not always have me."

Be completely open with Jesus.

# — LET DOWN YOUR HAIR —

Shortly before Jesus was crucified, a woman named Mary poured a bottle of expensive perfume on His feet. Then, in an even more daring act, she wiped His feet with her hair (John 12:3). Not only did Mary sacrifice what may have been her life's savings, but she also sacrificed her reputation. In that culture, respectable women never let down their hair in public. But true worship is not concerned with what others think of us (2 Samuel 6:21–22). To worship Jesus, Mary was willing to be thought of as immodest, perhaps even immoral.

Some of us may feel pressured to be perfect when we go to church. But in a healthy church, we can let down our hair and not hide our flaws behind a façade of perfection. In church we should be able to reveal our weaknesses to find strength rather than conceal our faults to appear strong.

Worship isn't behaving as if nothing's wrong; it's making sure everything's right—right with God and with one another. When our greatest fear is letting down our hair, perhaps our greatest sin is keeping it up.

*Julie*

What about Mary's worship pleased Jesus? How does God want us to come to Him in worship?

Mary took a pound of costly perfume made of pure nard, anointed Jesus' feet, and wiped them with her hair. The house was filled with the fragrance of the perfume.

JOHN 12:3 NRSV

Read John 12:1-8, and enter into the biblical story by imagining yourself as Mary. Use your five senses: Feel the weight and texture of the jar of perfume in your hands. What's the scent that rises up as you anoint Jesus? Do you hear the whispered voices of disapproval as you wipe Jesus's feet with your hair? How does Jesus receive your act of worship?

*Write*

Identify one way to "let down your hair" this week.

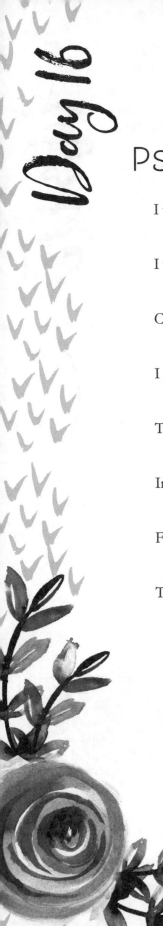

# PSALM 34:1-8 NLT

I will praise the LORD at all times.

    I will constantly speak his praises.

I will boast only in the LORD;

    let all who are helpless take heart.

Come, let us tell of the LORD's greatness;

    let us exalt his name together.

I prayed to the LORD, and he answered me.

    He freed me from all my fears.

Those who look to him for help will be radiant with joy;

    no shadow of shame will darken their faces.

In my desperation I prayed, and the LORD listened;

    he saved me from all my troubles.

For the angel of the LORD is a guard;

    he surrounds and defends all who fear him.

Taste and see that the LORD is good.

    Oh, the joys of those who take refuge in him!

# God wants me to *experience* Him, not just know about Him.

## — TASTE FOR YOURSELF —

A friend posted a Crock-Pot recipe on her Facebook page. The meal looked good, so I downloaded the recipe—intending to use it one day. Soon another friend was looking for similar meals, so I emailed her the recipe. She forwarded it to several friends, who passed it on as well.

Later I learned that the recipe had been forwarded far and wide though no one—not even the friend who posted it *originally*—had actually made the dish. We recommended it without having tasted it.

On occasion, we do something similar in matters of faith. While our motives to build "others up according to their needs" (Ephesians 4:29) are good and biblical, it's often easier to tell others' stories about trusting God than to exercise faith in Him ourselves.

God doesn't want me just to *talk* about Him; He wants me to *experience* Him.

Today may we taste for ourselves and see that God is good!

*Roxanne*

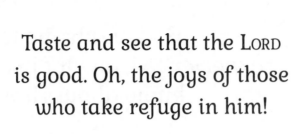

Taste and see that the LORD
is good. Oh, the joys of those
who take refuge in him!

PSALM 34:8 NLT

## CONNECT

What are some ways you experience God?

## PRAY

Play your favorite worship song during your quiet time with Jesus.

Imagine Scripture is like a Thanksgiving feast. To truly enjoy it, you don't want to inhale it but to eat slowly—savoring all its flavors. Today, as you read Psalm 34, read slowly. Discover a word or phrase that jumps out at you. Maybe "taste and see" (v. 8) or "radiant" (v. 5)? Stop. Take the rest of your quiet time to "taste" this one morsel of Scripture—and listen to God's word for you!

*Write*

# ROMANS 13:11-14

And do this, understanding the present time: The hour has already come for you to wake up from your slumber, because our salvation is nearer now than when we first believed. The night is nearly over; the day is almost here. So let us put aside the deeds of darkness and put on the armor of light. Let us behave decently, as in the daytime, not in carousing and drunkenness, not in sexual immorality and debauchery, not in dissension and jealousy. Rather, clothe yourselves with the Lord Jesus Christ, and do not think about how to gratify the desires of the flesh.

# I dress myself in Christ.

## Dressed Up

In her book *Wearing God*, author Lauren Winner says our clothes can silently communicate to others who we are. She writes, "The idea that, as with a garment, Christians might wordlessly speak something of Jesus—is appealing."

According to Paul, we too can wordlessly represent Christ. Romans 13:14 tells us to "clothe [ourselves] with the Lord Jesus Christ, and do not think about how to gratify the desires of the flesh." When we become Christians, we take on Christ's identity. We're "children of God through faith" (Galatians 3:26–27). That's our status. Yet each day we need to clothe ourselves in His character. We do this by striving to live for and to be more like Jesus, growing in godliness, love, and obedience and turning our back on the sins that once enslaved us.

This growth in Christ is a result of the Holy Spirit working in us and our desire to be closer to Him through study of the Word, prayer, and time spent in fellowship with other Christians (John 14:26). When others look at our words and attitudes, what statement are we making about Christ?

*Alyson*

Which characteristics of Jesus would you like to wear? What do you like about them?

**Clothe yourselves with the Lord Jesus Christ.**

ROMANS 13:14

With Jesus, take an inventory of your last week. How did you dress yourself in Christ? When did you neglect putting on His character? Be kind to yourself. Jesus is with you, no matter what you "wear," and can use each situation to bring you closer to Him.

*Write*

_____

_____

_____

_____

_____

_____

_____

_____

_____

**Think of one way you'd like to dress yourself in Christ this week.**

# ROMANS 8:31-39 NRSV

What then are we to say about these things? If God is for us, who is against us? He who did not withhold his own Son, but gave him up for all of us, will he not with him also give us everything else? Who will bring any charge against God's elect? It is God who justifies. Who is to condemn? It is Christ Jesus, who died, yes, who was raised, who is at the right hand of God, who indeed intercedes for us. Who will separate us from the love of Christ? Will hardship, or distress, or persecution, or famine, or nakedness, or peril, or sword? As it is written,

> "For your sake we are being killed all day long;
>     we are accounted as sheep to be slaughtered."

No, in all these things we are more than conquerors through him who loved us. For I am convinced that neither death, nor life, nor angels, nor rulers, nor things present, nor things to come, nor powers, nor height, nor depth, nor anything else in all creation, will be able to separate us from the love of God in Christ Jesus our Lord.

God's love will
never let me go.

## LOCKED INTO LOVE

In 2015 the city of Paris removed forty-five tons of padlocks from the railings of the Pont des Arts pedestrian bridge. As a romantic gesture, couples would etch their initials onto a lock, attach it to the railing, click it shut, and throw the key into the River Seine.

After this ritual was repeated thousands of times, the bridge could no longer bear the weight of so much "love." Eventually the city, fearing for the integrity of the bridge, removed the "love locks."

The locks were meant to symbolize everlasting love, but human love does not always last. Human love can be fickle.

But there's one constant and enduring love—the love of God. "Give thanks to the LORD, . . . his love endures forever," proclaims Psalm 106:1. The promises of God's unfailing and everlasting love are found throughout Scripture. The greatest proof of this love is Jesus's death so those who put their faith in Him can live eternally. Nothing will ever separate us from His love (Romans 8:38–39).

Fellow believer, praise God! We are locked into His love forever.

*Cindy*

## PRAY

Ask Jesus to help you grasp His unbreakable love for you.

Write

Imagine looking into Jesus's face, and He is returning your gaze. What is it like allowing Jesus to see you? Do you feel loved, vulnerable, beautiful? What is Jesus's expression as He looks into your face?

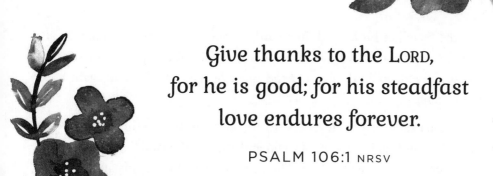

Give thanks to the LORD,
for he is good; for his steadfast
love endures forever.

PSALM 106:1 NRSV

## CONNECT

Remember a time you felt God's love for you when you missed the mark. What was it like to encounter His compassion in your weakness?

# JOSHUA 7:1-12 NRSV

But the Israelites broke faith in regard to the devoted things: Achan son of Carmi son of Zabdi son of Zerah, of the tribe of Judah, took some of the devoted things; and the anger of the LORD burned against the Israelites.

Joshua sent men from Jericho to Ai, which is near Beth-aven, east of Bethel, and said to them, "Go up and spy out the land." And the men went up and spied out Ai. Then they returned to Joshua and said to him, "Not all the people need go up; about two or three thousand men should go up and attack Ai. Since they are so few, do not make the whole people toil up there." So about three thousand of the people went up there; and they fled before the men of Ai. The men of Ai killed about thirty-six of them, chasing them from outside the gate as far as Shebarim and killing them on the slope. The hearts of the people melted and turned to water.

Then Joshua tore his clothes, and fell to the ground on his face before the ark of the LORD until the evening, he and the elders of Israel; and they put dust on their heads. Joshua said, "Ah, Lord GOD! Why have you brought this people across the Jordan at all, to hand us over to the Amorites so as to destroy us? Would that we had been content to settle beyond the Jordan! O Lord, what can I say, now that Israel has turned their backs to their enemies! The Canaanites and all the inhabitants of the land will hear of it, and surround us, and cut off our name from the earth. Then what will you do for your great name?"

The LORD said to Joshua, "Stand up! Why have you fallen upon your face? Israel has sinned; they have transgressed my covenant that I imposed on them. They have taken some of the devoted things; they have stolen, they have acted deceitfully, and they have put them among their own belongings. Therefore the Israelites are unable to stand before their enemies; they turn their backs to their enemies, because they have become a thing devoted for destruction themselves. I will be with you no more, unless you destroy the devoted things from among you."

When I acknowledge
my sin, I can be
made new.

# Destroying the Divides

A writing deadline loomed over me while a recent argument with my husband swirled through my mind. I stared at the blinking cursor, fingertips resting on the keyboard. *He was wrong too, Lord.*

When the computer screen went black, my reflection scowled. My unacknowledged wrongs were doing more than hindering my work. They were straining my relationship with my husband and my God. I grabbed my cell phone, swallowed my pride, and asked for forgiveness. Savoring the peace of reconciliation when my spouse apologized as well, I thanked God and finished my article on time.

The Israelites experienced the pain of personal sin and the joy of restoration. Joshua warned God's people not to enrich themselves in the battle for Jericho (Joshua 6:18), but Achan disobeyed (7:1). Only after his sin was exposed and dealt with (vv. 4–12) did the nation enjoy reconciliation with God.

Like Achan, we don't always consider how our sin turns our hearts from God and impacts others. Seeking forgiveness provides the foundation for healthy relationships with God and others. That's how we can enjoy His presence—together.

*Xochitl*

Create in me a pure heart,
O God, and renew a
steadfast spirit within me.

PSALM 51:10

## CONNECT

Today's reading reminds us that "seeking forgiveness provides the foundation for healthy relationships with God and others." How can offering your sin and burdens to God bring you closer to Him?

# PRAY

Confess your struggles to God, asking for freedom from unhealthy lifestyles and attitudes.

Open your Bible to Psalm 51, a confession King David wrote after committing adultery with Bathsheba. Feel David's grief as you read his raw, heartfelt words to God! Then rewrite Psalm 51 in your own words. What would you like to share with God in your version of Psalm 51?

Write

# Day 20

## 2 CORINTHIANS 1:3-7 NLT

All praise to God, the Father of our Lord Jesus Christ. God is our merciful Father and the source of all comfort. He comforts us in all our troubles so that we can comfort others. When they are troubled, we will be able to give them the same comfort God has given us. For the more we suffer for Christ, the more God will shower us with his comfort through Christ. Even when we are weighed down with troubles, it is for your comfort and salvation! For when we ourselves are comforted, we will certainly comfort you. Then you can patiently endure the same things we suffer. We are confident that as you share in our sufferings, you will also share in the comfort God gives us.

*I've been created to love wholeheartedly.*

## FULL-CIRCLE COMPASSION

Following a tumultuous season in her life, Bethany Haley Williams battled shame and brokenness. The journey was difficult, but through Jesus she experienced healing that transformed her life.

Prompted by the grace and mercy she received, Bethany formed Exile International, a nonprofit that implements art/expressive therapy and long-term, rehabilitative care to restore and empower war-affected children in Africa. Of her efforts, Bethany said, "When your greatest heartache becomes your greatest ministry, grace comes full circle."

Bethany now devotes her life to living out the words of 2 Corinthians 1:3–4. Having received God's comfort, she is now able to give others "the same comfort God has given [her]" (v. 4 NLT).

God knows about our suffering and misfortunes, and He is with us in the pain. He is merciful, loving, and attentive to our needs; and He can use whatever we experience to lift up and help others who are in need.

No matter what we've done or what we're facing, God is there to shower us with His compassion and love—gifts we can then share with others.

*Roxanne*

# PRAY

Together with Jesus, gently review the joys and disappointments of this season.

# CONNECT

Healing and transformation take time. Describe how God has brought you this far in your life. What battles has He helped you fight? What areas of your life do you still desire healing?

# Take Inventory

In today's reading, Bethany's experience with the transforming power of Jesus gave her the courage to help others by starting a nonprofit organization. List a few ways, big or small, that you can spread God's compassion.

\* ...................................................................

...................................................................

...................................................................

\* ...................................................................

...................................................................

\* ...................................................................

...................................................................

\* ...................................................................

...................................................................

...................................................................

\* ...................................................................

...................................................................

...................................................................

[God] comforts us in all our troubles so that we can comfort others. When they are troubled, we will be able to give them the same comfort God has given us.

2 CORINTHIANS 1:4 NLT

# PSALM 145:1-13

I will exalt you, my God the King;

 I will praise your name for ever and ever.

Every day I will praise you

 and extol your name for ever and ever.

Great is the LORD and most worthy of praise;

 his greatness no one can fathom.

One generation commends your works to another;

 they tell of your mighty acts.

They speak of the glorious splendor of your majesty—

 and I will meditate on your wonderful works.

They tell of the power of your awesome works—

 and I will proclaim your great deeds.

They celebrate your abundant goodness

 and joyfully sing of your righteousness.

The LORD is gracious and compassionate,

 slow to anger and rich in love.

The LORD is good to all;

 he has compassion on all he has made.

All your works praise you, LORD;

 your faithful people extol you.

They tell of the glory of your kingdom

 and speak of your might,

so that all people may know of your mighty acts

 and the glorious splendor of your kingdom.

Your kingdom is an everlasting kingdom,

 and your dominion endures through all generations.

    The LORD is trustworthy in all he promises

    and faithful in all he does.

*God has entrusted me
with a legacy of faith.*

## — GRANDMA'S RECIPE —

Many families have a secret recipe, a special way of cooking a dish that makes it especially savory. For us Hakkas (my Chinese ethnic group), we have a traditional dish called abacus beads, named for its beadlike appearance. Really, you have to try it!

Grandma had the best recipe. But we never got around to asking Grandma for it. She is no longer with us, and her secret recipe is gone with her.

We miss Grandma, and it's sad to lose her recipe. But far more tragic would be failing to preserve the legacy of faith entrusted to us. God intends that the mighty acts of God be shared from one generation to the next (Psalm 145:4). Moses had earlier instructed the Israelites to "remember the days of old. . . . Ask your father and he will tell you, your elders, and they will explain to you" (Deuteronomy 32:7).

As we share our stories of how we received salvation and the ways the Lord has helped us face challenges, we honor Him and pass the faith along. That is much more important than passing recipes along.

*Poh Fang*

Remember the days of old;
consider the generations long past.
Ask your father and he will tell you, your
elders, and they will explain to you.

DEUTERONOMY 32:7

# CONNECT

Who do you admire in your family or community, and what is this person's legacy? Identify one way you'd like to become like him or her.

Think about something you'd like to share with the next generation.

Take time to pray for the people you love. List several of their names here, and ask God how He is leading you to pray for them.

*Write*

# JOHN 4:9-14, 27-29 NRSV

The Samaritan woman said to him, "How is it that you, a Jew, ask a drink of me, a woman of Samaria?" (Jews do not share things in common with Samaritans.) Jesus answered her, "If you knew the gift of God, and who it is that is saying to you, 'Give me a drink,' you would have asked him, and he would have given you living water." The woman said to him, "Sir, you have no bucket, and the well is deep. Where do you get that living water? Are you greater than our ancestor Jacob, who gave us the well, and with his sons and his flocks drank from it?" Jesus said to her, "Everyone who drinks of this water will be thirsty again, but those who drink of the water that I will give them will never be thirsty. The water that I will give will become in them a spring of water gushing up to eternal life."

Just then his disciples came. They were astonished that he was speaking with a woman, but no one said, "What do you want?" or, "Why are you speaking with her?" Then the woman left her water jar and went back to the city. She said to the people, "Come and see a man who told me everything I have ever done! He cannot be the Messiah, can he?"

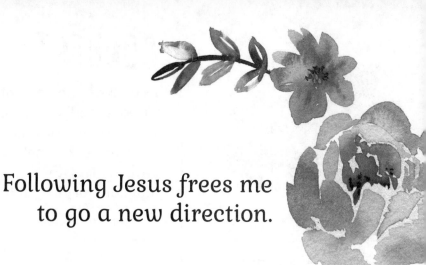

*Following Jesus frees me
to go a new direction.*

## LEAVING IT BEHIND

In the year or so after our teenage son got his driver's license and started carrying a wallet, we got several calls from people who had found it. We cautioned him to be more careful and not leave it behind.

Leaving things behind, though, is not always a bad thing. In John 4, we read about a woman who had come to draw water at a well. But after she encountered Jesus, her intent suddenly changed. Leaving her water jar behind, she hurried back to tell others what Jesus had said to her (vv. 28–29). Even her physical need for water faded in comparison to telling others about the Man she had just met.

Peter and Andrew did something that was similar when Jesus called them. They left their fishing nets (which was the way they earned their living) to follow Jesus (Matthew 4:18–20).

Our new life of following Jesus Christ may mean that we have to leave things behind, including those that don't bring lasting satisfaction. What we once craved cannot compare with the life and "living water" Jesus offers.

*Cindy*

# CONNECT

Jesus gave the Samaritan woman a new purpose, and she left everything behind to follow Him. How has Jesus given your life purpose? What would you like to leave behind to realize His dreams for you more fully?

Then the woman left her water jar and went back to the city. She said to the people, "Come and see a man who told me everything I have ever done! He cannot be the Messiah, can he?"

JOHN 4:28–29 NRSV

Read today's Bible passage again, and enter into the story by imagining that you are the Samaritan woman. What do you touch or taste as you collect water from the well? What smells waft from the village? See the stranger (Jesus) approaching the well. Talk to Him. What do you want Him to know? How do His words make you feel?

*Write*

........................................................................................................

........................................................................................................

........................................................................................................

........................................................................................................

........................................................................................................

........................................................................................................

........................................................................................................

........................................................................................................

........................................................................................................

## PRAY

Invite Jesus to share His dreams and desires for you.

## JOHN 13:33-35 NLT

Dear children, I will be with you only a little longer. And as I told the Jewish leaders, you will search for me, but you can't come where I am going. So now I am giving you a new commandment: Love each other. Just as I have loved you, you should love each other. Your love for one another will prove to the world that you are my disciples.

**Through Christ, I can experience healing even in a broken world.**

## SOMEONE TO TRUST

"I just can't trust anyone," my friend said through tears. "Every time I do, they hurt me." Her story angered me. An ex-boyfriend she thought she could trust had spread rumors about her when they broke up. As she struggled to trust again after a pain-filled childhood, this betrayal proved it to her: people can't be trusted.

Her story was painfully familiar, reminding me of moments of unexpected betrayal in my own life. In fact, Scripture is candid about human nature. In Proverbs 20:6, the author voices the same lament as my friend.

What I could say to her is that betrayal is only part of the story. Although wounds from others are real, Jesus has made genuine love possible. In John 13:35, Jesus told His disciples that others would know they were His followers because of their love. Yes, people may hurt us, but because of Jesus there will also always be those who share His love unconditionally. Resting in Christ's unfailing love, may we find healing, community, and the courage to love others as He did.

*Monica*

# Identify where you need restoration and healing.

Invite Jesus to lovingly view the damaged places of your heart, and ask for His healing.

Write

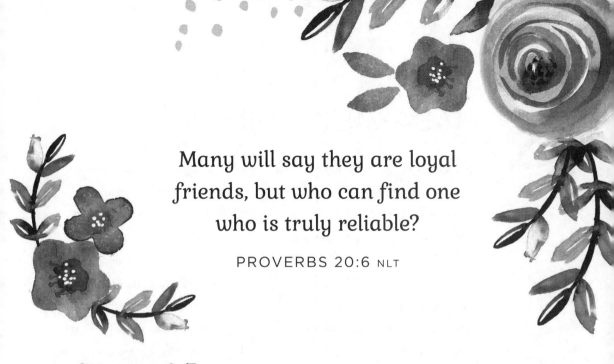

Many will say they are loyal
friends, but who can find one
who is truly reliable?

PROVERBS 20:6 NLT

## CONNECT

At some point in our lives, someone close to us has likely betrayed us.
While betrayal is part of the human story, it is not part of God's. Where
has God healed you and restored broken parts of your life?

# HABAKKUK 1:2-11 NLT

How long, O LORD, must I call for help?
　But you do not listen!
"Violence is everywhere!" I cry,
　but you do not come to save.
Must I forever see these evil deeds?
　Why must I watch all this misery?
Wherever I look,
　I see destruction and violence.
I am surrounded by people
　who love to argue and fight.
The law has become paralyzed,
　and there is no justice in the courts.
The wicked far outnumber the
　　righteous,
　so that justice has become perverted.
The LORD replied,
"Look around at the nations;
　look and be amazed!
For I am doing something in your own
　　day,
　something you wouldn't believe
　even if someone told you about it.

I am raising up the Babylonians,
　a cruel and violent people.
They will march across the world
　and conquer other lands.
They are notorious for their cruelty
　and do whatever they like.
Their horses are swifter than cheetahs
　and fiercer than wolves at dusk.
Their charioteers charge from far away.
　Like eagles, they swoop down to
　　devour their prey.
"On they come, all bent on violence.
　Their hordes advance like a desert
　　wind,
　sweeping captives ahead of them
　　like sand.
They scoff at kings and princes
　and scorn all their fortresses.
They simply pile ramps of earth
　against their walls and capture them!
They sweep past like the wind
　and are gone.
But they are deeply guilty,
　for their own strength is their god."

*God invites me to bring*
*my questions to Him.*

## How Long?

When I got married, I thought I would have children immediately. That did not happen, and the pain of infertility caused me to cry out to God, "How long?" I knew God could change my circumstance. Why didn't He?

Are you waiting on God? Are you asking, How long, Lord, before justice prevails in our world? Before there's a cure for cancer? Before I'm no longer in debt?

The prophet Habakkuk knew that feeling. In the seventh century BC, he cried out: "How long, Lord, must I call for help, but you do not listen? Or cry out to you, 'Violence!' but you do not save? . . . Why do you tolerate wrongdoing?" (1:2–3). He prayed, yet he struggled to reconcile how a just and powerful God could allow wickedness to continue in Judah. Why was God doing nothing?

There are days when we too feel as if God is doing nothing. Like Habakkuk, we ask God, "How long?"

We must continue to cast our burdens on the Lord because He cares for us. God hears us and will, in His time, give an answer.

*Karen*

# PRAY

Ask Jesus to pay attention to a specific need of yours— and listen for His response to you!

# CONNECT

When have you had to wait on God to fulfill a hope of yours? Did waiting for the dream to be realized make you want it more or less?

# Take Inventory

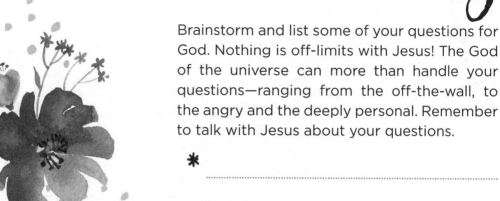

Brainstorm and list some of your questions for God. Nothing is off-limits with Jesus! The God of the universe can more than handle your questions—ranging from the off-the-wall, to the angry and the deeply personal. Remember to talk with Jesus about your questions.

*

*

How long,
O Lord,
must I call
for help?

HABAKKUK 1:2 NLT

*

*

*

# JOHN 15:1-5

I am the true vine, and my Father is the gardener. He cuts off every branch in me that bears no fruit, while every branch that does bear fruit he prunes so that it will be even more fruitful. You are already clean because of the word I have spoken to you. Remain in me, as I also remain in you. No branch can bear fruit by itself; it must remain in the vine. Neither can you bear fruit unless you remain in me.

I am the vine; you are the branches. If you remain in me and I in you, you will bear much fruit; apart from me you can do nothing.

## The pruning of my heart leads to growth.

# PAINFUL PRUNING

Last summer we planted rosebushes in the backyard in honor of my *abuelita*, my grandmother. Wild and sweet-smelling roses had grown around her house. The roses we planted would be a beautiful reminder of her.

I was joyful as I watched the roses bloom all summer. Then came the first frost. I knew it was time to lop off the roses and prune the branches.

Just as I had to prune the rosebushes to foster annual renewal, sometimes God needs to do some pruning in us. Even though it's painful and we don't welcome it, He prunes us so we "will be even more fruitful" (John 15:2). His aim isn't to hurt us, but to conform us into the image of Jesus (Romans 8:29) for our blessing and growth (Job 5:17).

Maybe you're going through a difficult time. You're struggling and wish the hurt and discomfort would go away. That's understandable. Yet, if you're being pruned, you can look to the future with great expectation. God is making sure you bear even more fruit. He'll never waste your pain and suffering.

*Marlena*

Where have you experienced God's pruning in your life? Was it painful? Did you grow as a result?

He cuts off every branch in me that bears no fruit, while every branch that does bear fruit he prunes so that it will be even more fruitful.

JOHN 15:2

How do you drink a cup of freshly brewed coffee on Saturday morning? You sip it slowly, enjoying its rich aroma, often curled up on the sofa (likely in your pajamas!). Today, enjoy Scripture in the same way. When you read the Bible passage, discover a phrase that jumps out at you—for example, "remain in me" (v. 4). Stop. "Get cozy" with this Scripture. Give yourself permission to spend the rest of your prayer time enjoying this one word or phrase. What is Jesus's invitation to you through it?

Identify how God may be pruning
your heart right now.

# ISAIAH 49:13-18 NRSV

Sing for joy, O heavens, and exult, O earth;

break forth, O mountains, into singing!

For the LORD has comforted his people,

and will have compassion on his suffering ones.

But Zion said, "The LORD has forsaken me,

my Lord has forgotten me."

Can a woman forget her nursing child,

or show no compassion for the child of her womb?

Even these may forget,

yet I will not forget you.

See, I have inscribed you on the palms of my hands;

your walls are continually before me.

Your builders outdo your destroyers,

and those who laid you waste go away from you.

Lift up your eyes all around and see;

they all gather, they come to you.

As I live, says the LORD,

you shall put all of them on like an ornament,

and like a bride you shall bind them on.

*God desires that I run to Him with all my needs.*

## No Need Is Too Trivial

Several mothers of small children were sharing encouraging answers to prayer. Yet one woman said she felt selfish about troubling God with her personal needs. "Compared with the huge global needs God faces," she explained, "my circumstances must seem trivial to Him."

Moments later, her little boy pinched his fingers in a door and ran screaming to his mother. She didn't say, "How selfish of you to bother me with your throbbing fingers when I'm busy!" Instead, she showed him great compassion and tenderness.

In Isaiah 49, God said that even though a mother may forget to have compassion on her child, the Lord never forgets His children (v. 15). God assured His people, "I have inscribed you on the palms of my hands" (v. 16 NRSV).

Such intimacy with God belongs to those who fear Him and who rely on Him rather than on themselves. As that child with throbbing fingers ran freely to his mother, so may we run to God with our daily problems.

Our compassionate God has limitless time and love for each of His children. No need is too trivial for Him.

*Joanie*

# PRAY

*Jesus, how amazing that you are always thinking about me, that I'm written on the palms of your hands (Isaiah 49:16).*

# CONNECT

Today's Scripture passages say God is like a loving parent. Where in your life do you need a parent's compassion? Imagine being a child and running to your Father in heaven, who looks at you with total acceptance—seeing your struggles and your needs.

# Take Inventory

God wants us to bring both our big requests and our daily needs to Him. What are some "trivial" things in your life that you can give to Jesus in prayer today?

As a father has compassion for his children, so the LORD has compassion for those who fear him.

PSALM 103:13 NRSV

\*

\*

\*

\*

\*

# 1 CORINTHIANS 15:42-58 NLT

It is the same way with the resurrection of the dead. Our earthly bodies are planted in the ground when we die, but they will be raised to live forever. Our bodies are buried in brokenness, but they will be raised in glory. They are buried in weakness, but they will be raised in strength. They are buried as natural human bodies, but they will be raised as spiritual bodies. For just as there are natural bodies, there are also spiritual bodies.

The Scriptures tell us, "The first man, Adam, became a living person." But the last Adam—that is, Christ—is a life-giving Spirit. What comes first is the natural body, then the spiritual body comes later. Adam, the first man, was made from the dust of the earth, while Christ, the second man, came from heaven. Earthly people are like the earthly man, and heavenly people are like the heavenly man. Just as we are now like the earthly man, we will someday be like the heavenly man.

What I am saying, dear brothers and sisters, is that our physical bodies cannot inherit the Kingdom of God. These dying bodies cannot inherit what will last forever.

But let me reveal to you a wonderful secret. We will not all die, but we will all be transformed! It will happen in a moment, in the blink of an eye, when the last trumpet is blown. For when the trumpet sounds, those who have died will be raised to live forever. And we who are living will also be transformed. For our dying bodies must be transformed into bodies that will never die; our mortal bodies must be transformed into immortal bodies.

Then, when our dying bodies have been transformed into bodies that will never die, this Scripture will be fulfilled:

"Death is swallowed up in victory.

O death, where is your victory?

O death, where is your sting?"

For sin is the sting that results in death, and the law gives sin its power. But thank God! He gives us victory over sin and death through our Lord Jesus Christ.

So, my dear brothers and sisters, be strong and immovable. Always work enthusiastically for the Lord, for you know that nothing you do for the Lord is ever useless.

## In Christ, everything I do has purpose.

# NOTHING IS USELESS

In my third year battling discouragement and depression caused by limited mobility and chronic pain, I confided to a friend, "My body's falling apart. I feel like I have nothing of value to offer God or anyone else."

"Would you say it doesn't make a difference when I greet you with a smile or listen to you?" she asked. "Would you tell me it's worthless when I pray for you?"

"Of course not."

"Then why are you telling yourself those lies? You do all those things for me and for others."

I thanked God for reminding me that nothing we do for Him is useless.

Because God promises we'll be resurrected through Christ (1 Corinthians 15:43), we can trust Him to use every small effort done for Him to make a difference in His kingdom (v. 58).

Even when we're physically limited, a smile, a word of encouragement, a prayer, or a display of faith during our trial can be used to minister to others. When we serve the Lord, no job or act of love is too menial to matter.

*Xochitl*

# CONNECT

Today's reading says, "When we serve the Lord, no job or act of love is too menial to matter." What is a simple task or job you do each day or week? How can you serve God as you carry it out?

Nothing
you do
for the Lord
is ever
useless.

1 CORINTHIANS 15:58

NLT

Take a few minutes in prayer to just let God love you! (If you need help getting started, try to picture Jesus's face—and He is smiling at you! How does that make you feel?) Journal about the experience.

*Write*

..........................................................................................................................

..........................................................................................................................

..........................................................................................................................

..........................................................................................................................

..........................................................................................................................

..........................................................................................................................

..........................................................................................................................

..........................................................................................................................

..........................................................................................................................

..........................................................................................................................

Thank someone for doing
behind-the-scenes work.

# Day 18

## HEBREWS 11:8-16

By faith Abraham, when called to go to a place he would later receive as his inheritance, obeyed and went, even though he did not know where he was going. By faith he made his home in the promised land like a stranger in a foreign country; he lived in tents, as did Isaac and Jacob, who were heirs with him of the same promise. For he was looking forward to the city with foundations, whose architect and builder is God. And by faith even Sarah, who was past childbearing age, was enabled to bear children because she considered him faithful who had made the promise. And so from this one man, and he as good as dead, came descendants as numerous as the stars in the sky and as countless as the sand on the seashore.

All these people were still living by faith when they died. They did not receive the things promised; they only saw them and welcomed them from a distance, admitting that they were foreigners and strangers on earth. People who say such things show that they are looking for a country of their own. If they had been thinking of the country they had left, they would have had opportunity to return. Instead, they were longing for a better country—a heavenly one. Therefore God is not ashamed to be called their God, for he has prepared a city for them.

I look forward to
my eternal home.

## STRANGERS AND FOREIGNERS

I parked my bicycle, fingering my map of Cambridge for reassurance. Directions not being my strength, I knew I could easily get lost in this maze of roads bursting with historic buildings.

Life should have felt idyllic, for I had just married my Englishman and moved to the United Kingdom. But I felt adrift. I didn't yet know what my role was as an American in Britain, and I realized that blending two stubborn people into one shared life was harder than I had anticipated.

I related to Abraham, who left everything to obey God and live as a stranger in a new land (Genesis 12:1). He pressed through the cultural challenges while keeping faith in God (Hebrews 11:9). Abraham lived by faith, longing for things promised, hoping and waiting for his heavenly home.

As Christ-followers we're all foreigners and strangers on this earth. By faith we press forward, knowing that God will lead and guide us, and by faith we believe He will never leave nor abandon us. By faith we long for home.

*Amy*

Identify a way God is growing your faith.

## CONNECT

Describe a time when you moved to a different town or were new to a team, club, or activity. What was it like to be an "outsider"?

# Take Inventory

As a follower of Jesus, heaven—not Earth—is your true home. What is exciting about heaven being your real home?

\* ................................................................
................................................................
................................................................

\* ................................................................
................................................................
................................................................

\* ................................................................
................................................................
................................................................

\* ................................................................
................................................................
................................................................

\* ................................................................
................................................................
................................................................

He was looking
forward to
the city with
foundations,
whose architect
and builder
is God.

HEBREWS 11:10

# Day 29

## LUKE 10:38-42

As Jesus and his disciples were on their way, he came to a village where a woman named Martha opened her home to him. She had a sister called Mary, who sat at the Lord's feet listening to what he said. But Martha was distracted by all the preparations that had to be made. She came to him and asked, "Lord, don't you care that my sister has left me to do the work by myself? Tell her to help me!"

"Martha, Martha," the Lord answered, "you are worried and upset about many things, but few things are needed—or indeed only one. Mary has chosen what is better, and it will not be taken away from her."

*Service and prayer
work together.*

# ⌐SERVING WITHOUT DISTRACTION¬

While Martha served Jesus unsparingly, her sister Mary sat at His feet, listening and learning. Commenting on this situation, Charles H. Spurgeon (1834–1892) wrote, "We should do much service and have much communion at the same time. For this we need great grace. It is easier to serve than to commune."

I once met a young mother who found the grace to do both. She hungered after God and His Word and was immersed deeply in family life each day. One day an idea came to her. In each room she placed paper and a pencil. As she served the Lord throughout the day in her home, she also kept herself open to God. Whenever a Scripture came to mind or something to confess or to pray about, she jotted it on the nearest pad of paper. In the evening after the children were asleep, she gathered her pieces of paper and pondered them prayerfully.

This woman found a way to be Martha and Mary at the same time. May we too discover ways to both serve God and commune with Him.

*Joanie*

## Identify a distraction in your life.

Enter into today's Bible story by imagining yourself as Martha or Mary. How do you react when you learn Jesus is coming for dinner? What's your relationship with Jesus? Are you close to Him or a casual acquaintance? As you talk with Jesus, what do you want Him to know? What does He want you to know?

*Write*

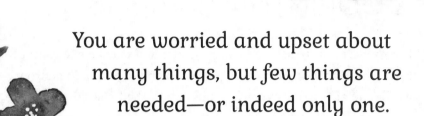

You are worried and upset about many things, but *few things are needed—or indeed only one.*

LUKE 10:41-42

# CONNECT

The young woman in today's reading found a way to balance serving others and spending time with God. What are some practical ways you can find this balance in your own life?

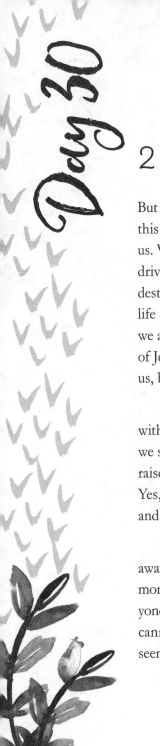

# Day 30

# 2 CORINTHIANS 4:7-18 NRSV

But we have this treasure in clay jars, so that it may be made clear that this extraordinary power belongs to God and does not come from us. We are afflicted in every way, but not crushed; perplexed, but not driven to despair; persecuted, but not forsaken; struck down, but not destroyed; always carrying in the body the death of Jesus, so that the life of Jesus may also be made visible in our bodies. For while we live, we are always being given up to death for Jesus' sake, so that the life of Jesus may be made visible in our mortal flesh. So death is at work in us, but life in you.

But just as we have the same spirit of faith that is in accordance with scripture—"I believed, and so I spoke"—we also believe, and so we speak, because we know that the one who raised the Lord Jesus will raise us also with Jesus, and will bring us with you into his presence. Yes, everything is for your sake, so that grace, as it extends to more and more people, may increase thanksgiving, to the glory of God.

So we do not lose heart. Even though our outer nature is wasting away, our inner nature is being renewed day by day. For this slight momentary affliction is preparing us for an eternal weight of glory beyond all measure, because we look not at what can be seen but at what cannot be seen; for what can be seen is temporary, but what cannot be seen is eternal.

# Even when I feel weak or helpless, God is powerful.

## NOZOMI HOPE

In 2011 a massive earthquake and tsunami took nearly 19,000 lives and destroyed 230,000 homes in northeastern Japan. In its aftermath, The Nozomi Project, named for the Japanese word for "hope," was created to provide sustainable income, community, and dignity—plus hope in a God who provides.

Nozomi women sift through the rubble to discover broken china shards that they turn into jewelry, which is sold around the world. This provides a livelihood for the women and shares symbols of their faith in Christ.

In New Testament times, people hid valuables in simple clay pots. Paul describes how the treasure of the gospel is contained in the human frailty of followers of Christ: jars of clay (2 Corinthians 4:7). He suggests that the meager—and even broken—vessels of our lives can reveal God's power in contrast to our imperfections.

When God inhabits the imperfect and broken pieces in our lives, the healing hope of His power is often made visible. No, His repair work in our hearts doesn't hide our imperfections. But perhaps those etchings in our beings make His character more visible to others.

*Elisa*

But we have this treasure in
clay jars, so that it may be made
clear that this extraordinary
power belongs to God and does
not come from us.

2 CORINTHIANS 4:7 NRSV

## CONNECT

Today's reading reminds us that when God is present in our lives, He brings powerful healing—to heart, body, and spirit—no matter how imperfect we may feel. Describe how God has healed you. How can your scars show others God's work in your life?

Praise God for His strength and power and invite Him to heal your broken places.

Write a letter to your 18-year-old self in which you share how God has moved in your life to provide restoration and healing in ways you could not have imagined.

*Write*

# Ephesians 4:1-6

As a prisoner for the Lord, then, I urge you to live a life worthy of the calling you have received. Be completely humble and gentle; be patient, bearing with one another in love. Make every effort to keep the unity of the Spirit through the bond of peace. There is one body and one Spirit, just as you were called to one hope when you were called; one Lord, one faith, one baptism; one God and Father of all, who is over all and through all and in all.

> God's heart is that I seek peace
> and unity in my relationships.

## — THE BOND OF PEACE —

After I confronted my friend by email over a matter on which we had differed, she didn't respond. Had I overstepped?

As she popped into my mind throughout the following days, I prayed for her, unsure of the way forward. Then one morning I went for a walk in our local park and saw her—pain etched on her face as she glimpsed me. "Thank you, Lord, that I can talk to her," I whispered as I approached her with a welcoming smile. We talked openly and were able to resolve matters.

Sometimes when hurt or silence intrudes on our relationships, mending them seems out of our control. But as the apostle Paul says in his letter to the church at Ephesus, we are called to work for peace and unity through God's Spirit—donning the garments of gentleness, humility, and patience as we seek God's healing in our relationships. The Lord yearns for us to be united, and through His Spirit He can bring His people together—even unexpectedly during a walk in the park.

*Amy*

# PRAY

Ask God to put a friend on your mind to pray for.

# CONNECT

In today's reading, Amy discussed friendships. Think about the friendships you have: Which friends would you like to spend more time with? Have you grown apart from a friend—but you'd like to renew the friendship?

# Take Inventory

Is there a great person that you would like to get to know better? How do you plan to reach out to him or her?

\*
.................................................................
.................................................................

\*
.................................................................
.................................................................

\*
.................................................................
.................................................................

\*
.................................................................
.................................................................

\*
.................................................................
.................................................................

Make every effort to keep the unity of the Spirit through the bond of peace.

EPHESIANS 4:3

# Day 31

## ISAIAH 40:1-8 NRSV

Comfort, O comfort my people,
   says your God.
Speak tenderly to Jerusalem,
   and cry to her
that she has served her term,
   that her penalty is paid,
that she has received from the LORD's hand
   double for all her sins.
A voice cries out:
"In the wilderness prepare the way of the LORD,
   make straight in the desert a highway for our God.
Every valley shall be lifted up,
   and every mountain and hill be made low;
the uneven ground shall become level,
   and the rough places a plain.
Then the glory of the LORD shall be revealed,
   and all people shall see it together,
   for the mouth of the LORD has spoken."
A voice says, "Cry out!"
   And I said, "What shall I cry?"
All people are grass,
   their constancy is like the flower of the field.
The grass withers, the flower fades,
   when the breath of the LORD blows upon it;
   surely the people are grass.
The grass withers, the flower fades;
   but the word of our God will stand forever.

*God's love toward me
is forever loyal.*

# FOREVER FLOWERS

One day when he was little, my son Xavier gave me a beautiful bouquet of artificial flowers. He grinned as he arranged the silk white calla lily, yellow sunflower, and purple hydrangea in a glass vase. "Look, Mommy," he said. "They'll last forever. That's how much I love you."

Since then my boy has grown into a young man. Those silk petals have frayed. The colors have faded. Still, the Forever Flowers remind me of his adoration. And there is something else it brings to mind—one thing that truly stands forever—the limitless and lasting love of God, as revealed in His infallible and enduring Word (Isaiah 40:8).

As the Israelites faced continual trials, Isaiah comforted them with confidence in God's enduring words. They trusted the prophet because his focus remained on God rather than their circumstances.

In a world filled with uncertainties and affliction, our feelings are ever shifting and as limited as our mortality (vv. 6–7). Still, we can trust God's unchanging love and character as revealed through His constant and eternally true Word.

*Xochitl*

## CONNECT

Today's reading says the Israelites trusted Isaiah "because his focus remained on God rather than their circumstances." As the Israelites did, we live in a world filled with uncertainty. How can you look to God for your security instead of relying on the things around you?

The grass withers,
the flower fades;
but the word
of our God will
stand forever.

ISAIAH 40:8 NRSV

Take inventory of the ways God has been faithful to you. Identify times Jesus has moved on your behalf through your circumstances, at your job, or in your relationships.

*Write*

.......................................................................................................

.......................................................................................................

.......................................................................................................

.......................................................................................................

.......................................................................................................

.......................................................................................................

.......................................................................................................

.......................................................................................................

.......................................................................................................

.......................................................................................................

**Identify one thing that has changed
in the last year.**

*Day 33*

# PSALM 131

My heart is not proud, LORD,

my eyes are not haughty;

I do not concern myself with great matters

or things too wonderful for me.

But I have calmed and quieted myself,

I am like a weaned child with its mother;

like a weaned child I am content.

Israel, put your hope in the LORD

both now and forevermore.

# I can rest in the arms of God.

## HELD BY GOD

As I neared the end of lunch with my sister and her children one afternoon, my sister told my three-year-old niece, Annica, it was time to get ready for her nap. Her face filled with alarm. "But Aunt Monica did not hold me yet today!" she objected, tears filling her eyes. My sister smiled. "Okay, she may hold you first—how long do you need?" "Five minutes," she replied.

As I held my niece, I was grateful for how, without even trying, she constantly reminds me what it looks like to love and be loved. I think we forget that our faith journey is one of learning to experience love—God's love—more fully than we can imagine (Ephesians 3:18).

Psalm 131 can help us to "become like little children" (Matthew 18:3) and let go of the battle in our mind over what we don't understand (Psalm 131:1). Through time with Him we can return to a place of peace (v. 2), finding the hope we need (v. 3) in His love—as calm and quiet as if we were children again in our mother's arms (v. 2).

*Monica*

# PRAY

Thank Jesus that you can come to Him in prayer just as you are.

## Write

Read Psalm 131 slowly. Is there a phrase that jumps out at you? Maybe it's "I have calmed and quieted myself" (v. 2) or "I am content" (v. 2)? Whatever the phrase, allow that particular Scripture to sink deeply into your heart. What is Jesus's invitation to you through it?

.................................................................................................

.................................................................................................

.................................................................................................

.................................................................................................

.................................................................................................

.................................................................................................

.................................................................................................

.................................................................................................

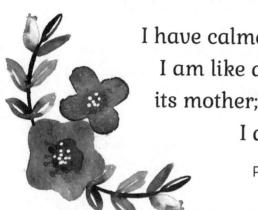

I have calmed and quieted myself,
I am like a weaned child with
its mother; like a weaned child
I am content.

PSALM 131:2

# CONNECT

Where do you need God's protection and provision? Take time to voice your needs to Him.

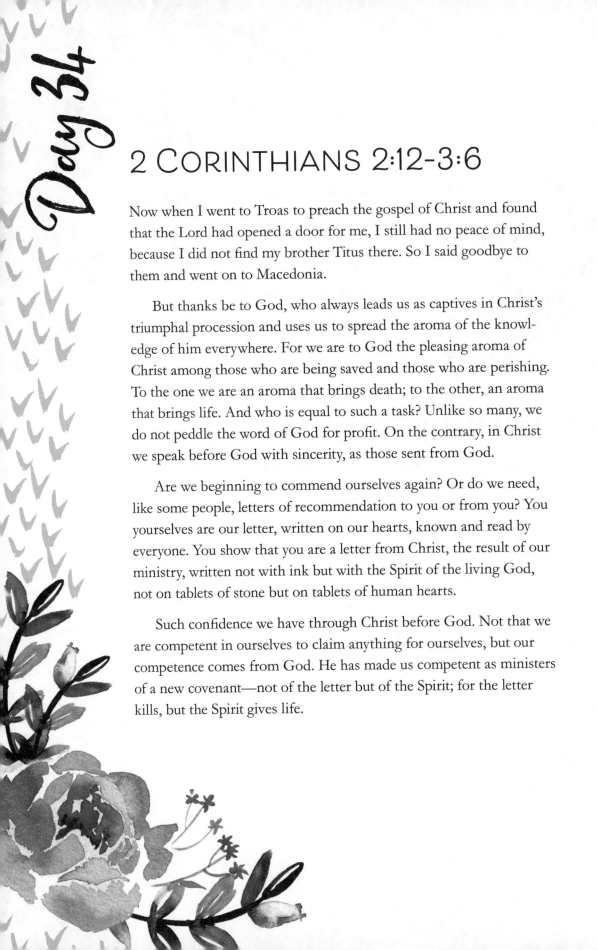

# Day 34

## 2 CORINTHIANS 2:12-3:6

Now when I went to Troas to preach the gospel of Christ and found that the Lord had opened a door for me, I still had no peace of mind, because I did not find my brother Titus there. So I said goodbye to them and went on to Macedonia.

But thanks be to God, who always leads us as captives in Christ's triumphal procession and uses us to spread the aroma of the knowledge of him everywhere. For we are to God the pleasing aroma of Christ among those who are being saved and those who are perishing. To the one we are an aroma that brings death; to the other, an aroma that brings life. And who is equal to such a task? Unlike so many, we do not peddle the word of God for profit. On the contrary, in Christ we speak before God with sincerity, as those sent from God.

Are we beginning to commend ourselves again? Or do we need, like some people, letters of recommendation to you or from you? You yourselves are our letter, written on our hearts, known and read by everyone. You show that you are a letter from Christ, the result of our ministry, written not with ink but with the Spirit of the living God, not on tablets of stone but on tablets of human hearts.

Such confidence we have through Christ before God. Not that we are competent in ourselves to claim anything for ourselves, but our competence comes from God. He has made us competent as ministers of a new covenant—not of the letter but of the Spirit; for the letter kills, but the Spirit gives life.

## My relationship with Jesus is fragrant.

# A MYSTERIOUS FRAGRANCE

Most of us can think of someone—perhaps a relative or a friend—who is known for a particular perfume she wears. Even without seeing her, we know when she's nearby. Wordlessly, her fragrance welcomes us into her company.

Every Christian should also be known for wearing a particular perfume—the fragrance of Christ. But it can't be bought at a cosmetic counter. It can't even be bottled and sold by the church. This mysterious perfume rises only out of our intimate relationship with Christ, and it wafts a subtle yet noticeable influence toward others.

Someone said about a Christian in his small town, "That woman never crosses my pathway without my being better for it!" Most likely, this admired believer had given a verbal witness at some point. But without the aroma of Christ, her witness would not have been effective.

The apostle Paul asked, "Who is equal to such a task" as exuding an aroma that brings life? (2 Corinthians 2:16). The answer? Our fragrance, our entire sufficiency, is from Christ alone. What fragrance will you be wearing today?

*Joanie*

Reflect on what it means to be a
"pleasing aroma of Christ."

## CONNECT

The fruits of the Spirit—"love, joy, peace, forbearance, kindness, good-ness, faithfulness, gentleness and self-control" (Galatians 5:22–23)—give off the aroma of Christ. What fruit of the Spirit has God been growing in you? How have you seen it at work in your life?

# Take Inventory

Who in your life gives off Christ's fragrance? Describe this person and the aroma.

For we are to God the pleasing aroma of Christ among those who are being saved and those who are perishing.

2 CORINTHIANS 2:15

* ......................................................
......................................................
......................................................

* ......................................................
......................................................
......................................................

* ......................................................
......................................................
......................................................

* ......................................................
......................................................
......................................................

* ......................................................
......................................................
......................................................

# PSALM 34:1-10 NLT

I will praise the LORD at all times.

  I will constantly speak his praises.

I will boast only in the LORD;

  let all who are helpless take heart.

Come, let us tell of the LORD's greatness;

  let us exalt his name together.

I prayed to the LORD, and he answered me.

  He freed me from all my fears.

Those who look to him for help will be radiant with joy;

  no shadow of shame will darken their faces.

In my desperation I prayed, and the LORD listened;

  he saved me from all my troubles.

For the angel of the LORD is a guard;

  he surrounds and defends all who fear him.

Taste and see that the LORD is good.

  Oh, the joys of those who take refuge in him!

Fear the LORD, you his godly people,

  for those who fear him will have all they need.

Even strong young lions sometimes go hungry,

  but those who trust in the LORD will lack no good thing.

# When anxious, I can turn to God for peace.

## FREE FROM FEAR

Fear sneaks into my heart without permission. It paints a picture of hopelessness and steals my peace. What am I fearful about? Safety of my family or the health of loved ones. The loss of a job or a broken relationship. Fear turns my focus inward and reveals an untrusting heart.

When these fears and worries strike, how good it is to read David's prayer in Psalm 34: "I sought the LORD, and he answered me; he delivered me from all my fears" (v. 4). And how does God deliver us from our fears? When we "look to him" (v. 5), we trust Him to be in control. Then David mentions a different type of fear—a deep respect and awe of the One who surrounds us and delivers us (v. 7). We can take refuge in Him because He is good (v. 8).

This awe of His goodness helps put our fears into perspective. When we remember who God is and how much He loves us, we can relax into His peace. In seeking the Lord we can be delivered from our fears.

*Keila*

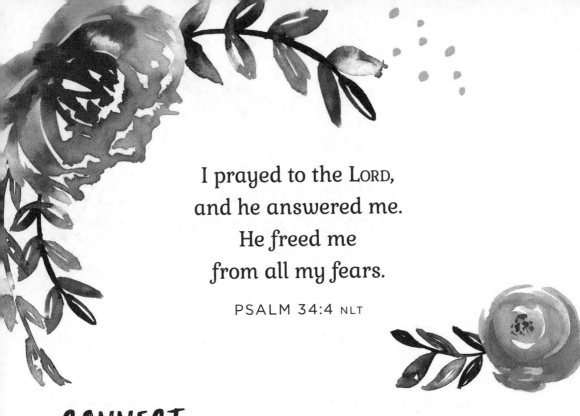

I prayed to the LORD,
and he answered me.
He freed me
from all my fears.

PSALM 34:4 NLT

## CONNECT

Has God ever rescued you when you cried out to Him? What did Jesus save you from?

## Name one thing that is causing you stress or anxiety.

In Psalm 34, the psalmist David desperately calls out to God. Where in your own life are you worried, discouraged, or heartbroken? Like David did, write your own psalm. In it, cry out to God for His protection and provision.

*Write*

........................................................................................................

........................................................................................................

........................................................................................................

........................................................................................................

........................................................................................................

........................................................................................................

........................................................................................................

........................................................................................................

........................................................................................................

........................................................................................................

# JOHN 14:15-26

"If you love me, keep my commands. And I will ask the Father, and he will give you another advocate to help you and be with you forever—the Spirit of truth. The world cannot accept him, because it neither sees him nor knows him. But you know him, for he lives with you and will be in you. I will not leave you as orphans; I will come to you. Before long, the world will not see me anymore, but you will see me. Because I live, you also will live. On that day you will realize that I am in my Father, and you are in me, and I am in you. Whoever has my commands and keeps them is the one who loves me. The one who loves me will be loved by my Father, and I too will love them and show myself to them."

Then Judas (not Judas Iscariot) said, "But, Lord, why do you intend to show yourself to us and not to the world?"

Jesus replied, "Anyone who loves me will obey my teaching. My Father will love them, and we will come to them and make our home with them. Anyone who does not love me will not obey my teaching. These words you hear are not my own; they belong to the Father who sent me.

"All this I have spoken while still with you. But the Advocate, the Holy Spirit, whom the Father will send in my name, will teach you all things and will remind you of everything I have said to you."

# God dwells within me.

## SWEET COMPANY

The elderly woman in the nursing home didn't speak to anyone or request anything. It seemed she merely existed, rocking in her creaky old chair. She didn't have many visitors, so one young nurse would often go into her room on her breaks. She didn't try to talk to the woman; she simply pulled up another chair and rocked with her. After several months, the elderly woman said to her, "Thank you for rocking with me." She was grateful for the companionship.

Before He went back to heaven, Jesus promised to send a constant companion to His disciples. He told them He would not leave them alone but would send the Holy Spirit (John 14:17). That promise is still true for believers in Jesus today. Jesus said that the triune God makes His "home" in us (v. 23).

The Lord is our close and faithful companion throughout our entire life. He will guide us in our deepest struggles, forgive our sin, hear each silent prayer, and shoulder the burdens we cannot bear.

We can enjoy His sweet company today.

*Anne*

# CONNECT

Jesus said the Holy Spirit lives in us. How have you experienced the power and comfort of the Holy Spirit?

The Spirit
of truth . . .
lives with you
and will
be in you.

JOHN 14:17

Stop. Take a deep breath. Quiet your heart—and listen: "Be still, and know that I am God" (Psalm 46:10). What is God inviting you to through His Word?

*Write*

........................................................................................

........................................................................................

........................................................................................

........................................................................................

........................................................................................

........................................................................................

........................................................................................

........................................................................................

........................................................................................

........................................................................................

## PRAY

Tell Jesus what you admire about Him—whether it's His character, creativity, kindness . . .

# HEBREWS 8:6-13 NLT

But now Jesus, our High Priest, has been given a ministry that is far superior to the old priesthood, for he is the one who mediates for us a far better covenant with God, based on better promises.

If the first covenant had been faultless, there would have been no need for a second covenant to replace it. But when God found fault with the people, he said:

"The day is coming, says the LORD,

when I will make a new covenant

with the people of Israel and Judah.

This covenant will not be like the one

I made with their ancestors

when I took them by the hand

and led them out of the land of Egypt.

They did not remain faithful to my covenant,

so I turned my back on them, says the LORD.

But this is the new covenant I will make

with the people of Israel on that day, says the LORD:

I will put my laws in their minds,

and I will write them on their hearts.

I will be their God,

and they will be my people.

And they will not need to teach their neighbors,

nor will they need to teach their relatives,

saying, 'You should know the LORD.'

For everyone, from the least to the greatest,

will know me already.

And I will forgive their wickedness,

and I will never again remember their sins."

When God speaks of a "new" covenant, it means he has made the first one obsolete. It is now out of date and will soon disappear.

In Christ, I am
wholly accepted.

# RINGS AND GRACE

When I look at my hands, I'm reminded that I lost my wedding and engagement rings. I was multitasking as I packed for a trip, and I still have no idea where they ended up.

I dreaded telling my husband about my careless mistake—worried how the news would affect him. But he responded with great compassion and care for me. While there are times when I still want to earn his grace, he doesn't hold this episode against me.

So many times we think of our sins and feel we must do something to earn God's forgiveness. But God has said it is by grace, not by works, that we are saved (Ephesians 2:8–9). We have a God who forgives and no longer calls to mind the wrongs we have done.

We may still feel sad about our past, but we need to trust God's promise. The grace and forgiveness that come through faith in Jesus Christ are real. Praise God, when God forgives, He forgets.

# PRAY

Ask Jesus to reveal the depth of His compassion toward you.

## Write

Thank Jesus for the way you are accepted, forgiven, and deeply loved.

..................................................................................................

..................................................................................................

..................................................................................................

..................................................................................................

..................................................................................................

..................................................................................................

..................................................................................................

..................................................................................................

..................................................................................................

..................................................................................................

..................................................................................................

..................................................................................................

I will never again
remember their sins.

HEBREWS 8:12 NLT

## CONNECT

Even though God has already forgiven us, sometimes we still strive to earn His love. What are ways you have tried to earn God's acceptance?

# LUKE 22:24-27 NLT

Then they began to argue among themselves about who would be the greatest among them. Jesus told them, "In this world the kings and great men lord it over their people, yet they are called 'friends of the people.' But among you it will be different. Those who are the greatest among you should take the lowest rank, and the leader should be like a servant. Who is more important, the one who sits at the table or the one who serves? The one who sits at the table, of course. But not here! For I am among you as one who serves."

*If Jesus served others, I want to follow in His footsteps.*

# ONE WHO SERVES

"I'm nobody's servant!" I cried out. That morning the demands of my family seemed too much as I frantically helped find my husband's blue tie while feeding the crying baby and recovering the lost toy from under the bed for our two-year-old.

Later that day, I came across something Jesus said, "For who is greater, the one who is at the table or the one who serves? Is it not the one who is at the table? But I am among you as one who serves" (Luke 22:27).

Today's society insists that we should aim to "be somebody." We want the best-paying job, the highest position in the company, an important role at church. Yet whatever position we are in, we can learn about service from our Savior.

We all hold different roles, but here's the question: Do we carry out those roles with an attitude of service? Even though my everyday routine is sometimes tiring, I'm thankful the Master helps me, because I want to follow His steps and willingly serve others.

May God help each of us be one who serves.

*Keila*

Who is more important,
the one who sits at the table
or the one who serves? The one who
sits at the table, of course. But not here!
For I am among you as one
who serves.

LUKE 22:27 NLT

# CONNECT

If Jesus led a business or church today, what would His leadership look like (Luke 22:24–27)? Would it be radically different from today's leadership? Why or why not?

## PRAY

Thank the God of the universe for the humble, radical way He came to serve us.

What are some ways you feel called to serve at your church, in your home, or in your community?

*Write*

..............................................................................................

..............................................................................................

..............................................................................................

..............................................................................................

..............................................................................................

..............................................................................................

..............................................................................................

..............................................................................................

..............................................................................................

..............................................................................................

..............................................................................................

# MARK 4:35-41

That day when evening came, he said to his disciples, "Let us go over to the other side." Leaving the crowd behind, they took him along, just as he was, in the boat. There were also other boats with him. A furious squall came up, and the waves broke over the boat, so that it was nearly swamped. Jesus was in the stern, sleeping on a cushion. The disciples woke him and said to him, "Teacher, don't you care if we drown?"

He got up, rebuked the wind and said to the waves, "Quiet! Be still!" Then the wind died down and it was completely calm.

He said to his disciples, "Why are you so afraid? Do you still have no faith?"

They were terrified and asked each other, "Who is this? Even the wind and the waves obey him!"

*Christ offers me security
in life's storms.*

# THE GIFT OF SLEEP

She told me she was depressed—extremely depressed.

It's hard to know what to say in such situations, so we talked about several things—medication, relationships with others and with God, and her habits. We agreed that if she could begin to sleep well, it would help her feel better emotionally and physically.

A lack of rest can make handling the challenges of life difficult. When it comes to sleep, I'm always fascinated that Jesus slept on a boat in the midst of a raging storm (Mark 4:38). *How could He do that?* The disciples didn't get it either. But the psalmist points to an answer: [God] "grants sleep to those he loves" (Psalm 127:2). Even in our struggle to rest, God is with us. We can rest in Him even when our eyes refuse to stay shut.

During those times, may we learn to "cast [our] cares on the LORD" (Psalm 55:22). As we do, we *can* choose to wait confidently for the gift of rest He alone can provide (Psalm 127:2).

*Marlena*

157

# CONNECT

In Mark 4:35–41, Jesus and the disciples are out at sea—and remarkably Jesus sleeps during a storm! Have you ever experienced your own storm where Jesus seemed "asleep," unaware of your situation? Talk with Jesus about it.

Cast your cares on the Lord and he will sustain you.

PSALM 55:22

Read Mark 4:35–41 again, and enter into the biblical story by imagining yourself as a disciple caught in the storm with Jesus. What do you taste and touch? What is the smell of the sea? Imagine how you would feel during the storm—and as Jesus calms it. What is God's invitation to you through the story?

*Write*

........................................................................................

........................................................................................

........................................................................................

........................................................................................

........................................................................................

........................................................................................

........................................................................................

........................................................................................

........................................................................................

Take inventory on whether you have
had enough rest this week.

# GENESIS 18:1-15 NLT

The LORD appeared again to Abraham near the oak grove belonging to Mamre. One day Abraham was sitting at the entrance to his tent during the hottest part of the day. He looked up and noticed three men standing nearby. When he saw them, he ran to meet them and welcomed them, bowing low to the ground.

"My lord," he said, "if it pleases you, stop here for a while. Rest in the shade of this tree while water is brought to wash your feet. And since you've honored your servant with this visit, let me prepare some food to refresh you before you continue on your journey."

"All right," they said. "Do as you have said."

So Abraham ran back to the tent and said to Sarah, "Hurry! Get three large measures of your best flour, knead it into dough, and bake some bread." Then Abraham ran out to the herd and chose a tender calf and gave it to his servant, who quickly prepared it. When the food was ready, Abraham took some yogurt and milk and the roasted meat, and he served it to the men. As they ate, Abraham waited on them in the shade of the trees.

"Where is Sarah, your wife?" the visitors asked.

"She's inside the tent," Abraham replied.

Then one of them said, "I will return to you about this time next year, and your wife, Sarah, will have a son!"

Sarah was listening to this conversation from the tent. Abraham and Sarah were both very old by this time, and Sarah was long past the age of having children. So she laughed silently to herself and said, "How could a worn-out woman like me enjoy such pleasure, especially when my master—my husband—is also so old?"

Then the LORD said to Abraham, "Why did Sarah laugh? Why did she say, 'Can an old woman like me have a baby?' Is anything too hard for the LORD? I will return about this time next year, and Sarah will have a son."

Sarah was afraid, so she denied it, saying, "I didn't laugh."

But the LORD said, "No, you did laugh."

# God will fulfill His purpose through me.

## NEVER TOO OLD

The women of Brown Manor had raised their families and retired from their careers. Now they could no longer live on their own, so they came to Brown Manor as a sort of "last stop before heaven." They enjoyed each other's company but struggled with feelings of uselessness.

One of the women, who had spent years playing the piano, often played hymns on the manor's piano. Other women joined her, and together they lifted their voices in praise to God.

One day a government auditor was conducting an inspection during one of their spontaneous worship services. When he heard them sing "What Will You Do with Jesus?" he recalled the song from his childhood. That day, God spoke to him again, and this time he trusted Jesus.

Like the women of Brown Manor, Sarah thought she was too old to be used by God (Genesis 18:11). But God gave her a child in her old age who was the ancestor of Jesus (21:1–3; Matthew 1:2, 17). Like Sarah and the women of Brown Manor, we're never too old for God to use us.

*Julie*

# PRAY

*Is anything too hard for You, Jesus (Genesis 18:14)? Help me trust that You can do far more than I ask or imagine (Ephesians 3:20).*

# CONNECT

In today's Bible passage, the matriarch Sarah believes her dream of having a child dies as she ages. Are there any dreams of yours past their expiration date? Take a few minutes to share them with God and hear what He has to say about them.

# Take Inventory

Reflect on the ways God has worked throughout your life. List a few of them here.

*  ................................................................
   ................................................................
   ................................................................

*  ................................................................
   ................................................................
   ................................................................
   ................................................................

*  ................................................................
   ................................................................
   ................................................................

*  ................................................................
   ................................................................
   ................................................................
   ................................................................

*  ................................................................
   ................................................................
   ................................................................
   ................................................................

Is anything too hard for the LORD? I will return about this time next year, and Sarah will have a son.

GENESIS 18:14 NLT

Now that you've concluded your 40-day journey, what have you learned about God, His character, and His love for you?

................................................................................

................................................................................

................................................................................

................................................................................

................................................................................

................................................................................

................................................................................

................................................................................

................................................................................

................................................................................

# MORE FROM
## *GOD HEARS HER*

FOREWORD BY LIZ CURTIS HIGGS

*God Sees Her*

365 Devotions
for Women by Women

Our Daily Bread

FOREWORD BY ELISA MORGAN

*God Hears Her*

365 Devotions
for Women by Women

Our Daily Bread

PRÓLOGO DE ELISA MORGAN

*Dios te escucha*

365 devocionales para mujeres
escritos por mujeres

Nuestro Pan Diario

# DEVOTIONALS TO MEET YOUR NEEDS

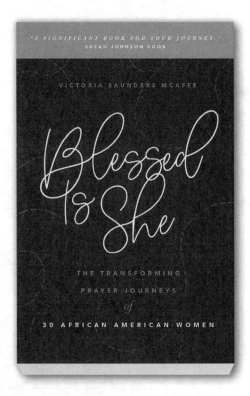

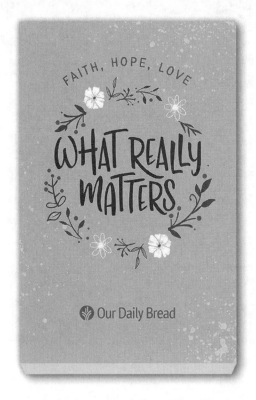

# If you appreciated *God Hears Her 40-Day Devotional Journal*, please let others know.

- Pick up another copy to give as a gift.

- Share a link to the book or mention it on social media.

- Write a review on your blog, on a bookseller's website, or at our own site (odb.org/store).

- Recommend this book for your church, book club, or small group.

## Contact us to share your thoughts.

**godhearsher.org**

☐ @godhearsher

☐ @godhearsher

☐ @godhearsher

Our Daily Bread Publishing
PO Box 3566
Grand Rapids, Michigan 49501 USA

✉ books@odb.org